The Distance Learner's Guide

Second Edition

Western Cooperative for Educational Telecommunications

Editors
Sally M. Johnstone & George P. Connick

wcet

The Cooperative advancing the effective use of technology in higher education

PEARSON
Merrill
Prentice Hall

Upper Saddle River, New Jersey
Columbus, Ohio

Library of Congress Cataloging in Publication Data
The distance learner's guide / Western Cooperative for Educational
Telecommunications; editors, Sally M. Johnstone & George P. Connick. -- 2nd ed.
    p. cm.
  Includes index.
  ISBN 0-13-114540-1
  1. Distance education. 2. Distance education--Computer-assisted instruction.
I. Johnstone, Sally (Sally M.) II. Connick, George P. III. Western Cooperative
for Educational Telecommunications.

  LC5800.D578 2005
  371.35--dc22

                                          2004008922

Editor in Chief: Jeffery W. Johnston
Senior Acquisitions Editor: Sande Johnson
Editorial Assistant: Erin Anderson
Production Editor: Holcomb Hathaway
Design Coordinator: Diane C. Lorenzo
Cover Designer: Jeff Vanik
Production Manager: Pamela D. Bennett
Director of Marketing: Ann Castel Davis
Marketing Manager: Eric Murray
Marketing Coordinator: Tyra Poole

This book was set in Palatino by Carlisle Communications, Ltd. It was printed and bound
by Courier Westford, Inc. The cover was printed by The Lehigh Press, Inc.

Pearson Education Ltd.
Pearson Education Singapore Pte. Ltd.
Pearson Education Canada, Ltd.
Pearson Education—Japan

Pearson Education Australia Pty. Limited
Pearson Education North Asia Ltd.
Pearson Educación de Mexico, S.A. de C.V.
Pearson Education Malaysia Pte. Ltd.

BK
$21.36

10 9 8 7 6 5 4 3 2 1
ISBN: 0-13-114540-1

CONTENTS

1 — DISTANCE LEARNING

Foreword

Since the first edition of this guide was published in 1999, the number of college courses offered to students on the Internet and World Wide Web has increased exponentially. The Western Cooperative for Educational Telecommunications (WCET) works to encourage these sorts of opportunities for students. It also works with colleges and universities to ensure that the students who choose to study electronically receive not only high-quality instruction, but also good support services. As part of that effort, we suggest that colleges and universities begin to think about students as consumers of educational services and give them the level of service that consumers should expect.

As colleges and universities begin to treat students as consumers, it is critical that the students understand how to be informed consumers. That is what this book is all about. Through many years of research and interviews with students and their instructors, we know that students studying in an electronic environment must take more control over their learning than might be the case for students in a face-to-face class.

This book is designed to empower students and to help them understand how to be informed consumers of electronically mediated learning and, consequently, more successful in this new environment.

Sally M. Johnstone, Executive Director
WCET
Western Cooperative for Educational Telecommunications

Preface

This guide is designed to help you reach your educational goals. It is about a world of higher education that is new; expanding rapidly; and can be accessed from home, work, or other locations distant from a campus. In other words, it is about what is termed *distance learning*.

Whereas the traditional college experience takes place on a campus at specific times each week, you, as a distance learner, will access your courses in a "virtual educational world" at times and places convenient to you.

Distance learning has expanded dramatically as a result of amazing developments in computers, telecommunications, the Internet, and the World Wide Web. The merging of these technologies has resulted in an "information technology revolution" and has made possible the rapid expansion of distance learning options. Today, distance learning is a new educational culture with its own distinct characteristics.

As you search for distance learning opportunities, you will find this guide valuable in several important ways.

First, it is designed to help you understand and successfully navigate every avenue of this new "virtual culture" in higher education. Written by experts in distance learning, each chapter is full of detailed information about degree programs and services available at a distance.

Second, it is the first book that provides comprehensive guidance in the areas essential for success in distance learning. It will help you determine which distance education provider is right for you, use a computer for distance learning, access library resources from a distance, and secure a wide range of student services without traveling to a campus.

Finally, it is much more than a book. It is a dynamic learning tool, combining the book with the interactive capabilities of the Internet and the World Wide Web. The website directs you to locations on the Web where there is supplementary material for the chapters. Because the website is routinely updated, the book remains current.

The back cover of the first edition of this book included an illustration of Aesop's 2,500-year-old fable "The Hare and the Tortoise." As you will recall, the tortoise and the hare argued about who could run faster. The hare challenged the tortoise to a race. At the beginning of the race, the hare quickly took the lead and became bored. He stopped to rest and soon fell asleep. The tortoise plodded along without stopping, focused on her goal. Just as the hare awoke, the tortoise crossed the finish line. The moral of this fable is "slow and steady wins the race." This lesson also applies to education. There are no shortcuts and no instant returns on your educational investment.

Acknowledgments

This guide was the brainchild of a team of people who realized the time had come to help students know what questions they needed to ask when selecting a distance learning provider. That team consisted of George Connick, Barbara Krauth, Russell Poulin, and Sally Johnstone. George took on the task of editing the first edition of the guide, for which we were all grateful. The individual authors of the chapters agreed to work together without individual ownership of their work. They dedicated their efforts to the broader goals of the Western Cooperative for Educational Telecommunications as it tries to help higher education institutions offer students the best service possible.

A number of reviewers made valuable suggestions for improving this edition. We would like to thank H. Draper Hunt, Professor Emeritus of the University of Southern Maine, Portland; Ellen Wagner, Director of Higher Education at Macromedia, San Francisco; Robert Threlkeld, former Dean at California State University, Fresno; Steve Tilson, former Director of Learning at US Open University, Denver; Alfredo G. de los Santos Jr., Senior Fellow at League of Innovation, Tempe, Arizona; Butch Gemin, Director of Business Development at the Monterey Institute for Technology and Education; and Ron Baker, Deputy Executive Director at Northwest Commission of Schools & Colleges, Redmond, Washington.

We are indebted to Sherri Artz Gilbert and Rachel Sonntag, staff at the Western Cooperative for Educational Telecommunications, who provided enormous assistance by coordinating deadlines and numerous mailings among authors and handling the multitude of details necessary to bring this book to completion.

A special thanks to the members of the Western Cooperative for Educational Telecommunications for their support of the collective efforts that are reflected in this book. Further information about WCET's activities can be found at **www.wcet.info·**

Contributing Authors

David Bilyeu (Chapter 4) is college librarian at Central Oregon Community College in Bend, Oregon. He serves on many regional library councils working on distance education and academic library consortium issues throughout Oregon and Washington. David has consulted with the Western Interstate Commission for Higher Education in planning for library services for online university projects. He has held positions at Caltech in Pasadena, Cabrillo College in Santa Cruz, and Westmont College in Santa Barbara, California. He has a B.A. in philosophy from the University of California, Santa Cruz, and a master's degree in library and information science from Syracuse University.

Susan M. Campbell (Chapter 5) is executive director of the Division of Advising and Academic Resources at the University of Southern Maine. She received her B.S. in speech and theater from Ball State University, her M.S. in adult education from the University of Southern Maine, and her Ed.D. from the University of Massachusetts at Amherst. Susan has more than 25 years of experience in academic and student affairs administration and has held administrative positions in financial aid, admissions, summer session, and off-campus education. She teaches undergraduate courses in student leadership and graduate courses in both organizational management and student affairs. Her research and practice interests include student development, adult learning, enrollment management, academic advising, and career planning.

George P. Connick (Chapter 2) is the founder and president emeritus of the Education Network of Maine, the statewide distance learning network of the University of Maine System. During his 31-year association with the University of Maine System, he held various faculty and administrative positions, including nine years as the president of the University of Maine at Augusta (1985–94) and three years as president of the Education Network of Maine (1994–97). He has delivered more than 300 presentations on the uses of technology and telecommunications for distance learning, and he is the author of numerous articles and reports on a variety of educational topics. George is currently the president of Memory Lane Publications, a publishing company he founded in 2000. He also serves as a consultant to numerous higher education institutions in the United States and Canada on issues related to distance education. He earned his B. A. from Stanford University, his M. A. from San Jose State University, and his Ph. D. in history from the University of Colorado at Boulder.

Joseph Hart (Chapter 6) is the director of Special Programs in the Division of Distance Education at Eastern Oregon University. He received his B. A. in psychology from Lewis and Clark College, his M. S. in clinical psychology from the University of Wisconsin, and his Ph. D. in experimental psychology from Stanford University. He has taught and served as an academic administrator on the faculties of the University of California, Irvine; the University of Southern California; the University of Redlands, Whitehead Center; and the California State Polytechnic University in Pomona. He received an outstanding faculty teaching award at the University of Redlands for his work with adult students. Joe has written a variety of monographs, chapters, and articles on a range of subjects, which have appeared in various scientific journals. He has been involved with computer-mediated instruction since the early 1970s. His current work is focused on the development and use of online instructional resources; he maintains the EduResources Portal at **http://sage.eou:edu/SPT** and the EduResources Weblog at **http://radio.weblogs.com/0114870/**.

Fred Hurst (Chapter 3) is vice president for Extended Programs and dean of Distance Learning at Northern Arizona University (NAU) in Flagstaff. He has 24 years of experience in higher education, distance learning, and technology. Most recently, he has led an aggressive effort within NAU to expand distance learning programs and opportunities that utilize a variety of delivery mediums, including the Internet/Web, interactive videoconference, satellite television, and traditional face-to-face courses. As a result, NAU now has distance learning enrollments of more than 6,000 students each semester. Fred was dean of Information Technologies and Telecommunications for the Education Network of Maine. He was also the founding executive director of the Florida Public Postsecondary Distance Learning Institute and Florida Virtual Campus created by the State University and Community College Systems of Florida. Fred is an accomplished writer and presenter and has degrees in public administration, education, and telecommunications.

Sally M. Johnstone (editor) is the executive director of WCET, the Cooperative advancing the effective use of technology in higher education. WCET's members are colleges, universities, state agencies, educational associations, and corporations from throughout the United States and the world. Sally has worked with technology enhanced teaching and learning for over two decades. She leads national and international projects and has written dozens of articles on distance learning issues. She earned her Ph.D. in experimental psychology from the University of North Carolina, Chapel Hill.

Barbara Krauth (Chapter 1) is currently a consultant in the field of distance learning. She previously served as project director of two major distance learning projects at the Western Cooperative for Educational Telecommunications. Barbara leads a double professional life. In addition to her work in higher education, she is a consultant and researcher in the field of criminal justice. She has a B.A. in English from Indiana University; has graduate hours in public administration at the University of Colorado; and an M.A. in English literature from the University of Kent, Canterbury, England.

John Witherspoon (Chapter 4) is professor emeritus and former chair of telecommunications and film in the School of Communication, San Diego State University. A planner and consultant in telecommunication, he specializes in applications of communication technology for education and public service. He is the author of *Distance Education: A Planner's Casebook,* intended to assist higher education administrators as they look beyond the campus-bound university. John was founding chairman of the steering committee of the Western Cooperative for Educational Telecommunications as well as the Board of Directors of National Public Radio. He was also president of the Public Service Satellite Consortium; the first principal executive for television of the Corporation for Public Broadcasting; vice president of KCET Los Angeles; and the first general manager of KPBS-TV/FM, San Diego's public broadcasting stations.

CHAPTER 1

DISTANCE LEARNING

College Comes to You

In this chapter you will

- ◆ learn how to use this Guide
- ◆ learn about the concept of distance learning
- ◆ become familiar with some terms used to discuss distance learning
- ◆ discover some reasons why people are taking advantage of distance learning to meet their goals
- ◆ learn what it might be like to experience a distance learning course
- ◆ find out more about how the quality of distance learning is likely to compare with that of a traditional learning experience
- ◆ be given some tools to help you evaluate whether distance learning is for you

THE PURPOSE OF THE GUIDE

This book is a comprehensive guide to the world of distance learning. It is designed to provide you with a broad understanding of distance learning and to point to some issues that are key to your success as a distance learner. Unlike a novel, it is not designed to be read from cover to cover in one sitting, but we believe you will find it compelling reading as you explore the issues essential to your future success as a distance learner.

ORGANIZATION OF THE GUIDE

The Guide is organized into four sections. These sections represent the stages through which students pass as they access distance learning opportunities:

1. Chapter 1 introduces you to distance learning. It discusses terms and concepts that are at the core of the distance learning experience.
2. Chapters 2 through 4 focus on the academic issues that are essential to your success as a distance learner—how to choose the institution that best fits your personal needs, how to ensure that you have the appropriate technology, and how to access online libraries and other learning resources.
3. Chapters 5 and 6 cover the range of student support issues that are extremely important to the success of every distance learner. These chapters also discuss some online resources that can help you improve your performance. We often underestimate the importance of personal issues in our ultimate success as learners. If our personal lives are not in order, it is much more difficult to succeed in the highly structured world of education.

WHAT IS DISTANCE LEARNING?

A reasonable first question. The term *distance learning* is heard everywhere, but it's hard to know exactly what it is because it is defined in different ways. Perhaps the simplest definition is that distance learning takes place when the instructor and student are not in the same room but are separated by physical distance.

But the "distance" in the term doesn't imply any particular degree of separation. You can be a distance learner located only a short hop across campus from the instructor, or you can be thousands of miles away—across the continent or in another country. Whatever the physical space between the student and teacher, they are connected to each other by video, voice, or computer technologies.

Distance learning is a flexible form of education because it creates options in terms of where and when you can learn. As a distance learner, you may learn with others in a group gathered in a classroom at an off-campus site, or you may learn on your own from your computer at home, communicating with other students and your instructor only in a "virtual" space.

OTHER TERMS FOR DISTANCE LEARNING

- *Distance education* is a term that is often used interchangeably with *distance learning*. When you think about it, though, distance learning might best be seen as what takes place *as a result of* distance education.
- *e-Learning* is a term that has recently become prominent. It is often used to describe programs in which courses are taught online and that encourage collaboration and virtual interaction among students in the same course.
- The terms *online education, distributed education,* and *virtual education* are also sometimes used.

WHO OFFERS DISTANCE LEARNING PROGRAMS?

Many kinds of "providers" are offering distance learning programs. In addition to traditional colleges and universities, these providers include small and large businesses, government agencies, nonprofit organizations, and for-profit entities formed specifically to offer distance learning opportunities.

This handbook is designed especially for students interested in distance learning opportunities that are made available through traditional higher education institutions, both public and private:

- community colleges
- four-year colleges

- universities that award four-year and graduate and professional degrees
- consortia comprising groups of higher education institutions

ONLINE AND VIRTUAL UNIVERSITIES

The terms *virtual university* and *online university* sometimes turn up when distance learning is discussed. What are these institutions? Are they real places?

- An *online university* is likely to be an offshoot of a traditional institution. Remember, however, that it takes more than a home page on the Web to make an online university. An online university offers all its courses and programs via the Internet or World Wide Web. Examples are the Distance Learning Program (DIAL) of the New School for Social Research and the online branch of the University of Phoenix.
- A *virtual university* is a stand-alone institution that offers courses only at a distance. Jones International University, National Technological University, and Capella University are examples of virtual universities.

WHY STUDY AT A DISTANCE?

Students enroll in distance learning programs for a variety of reasons. Usually they are interested in the convenience such programs offer—the possibility of earning college credit at home, at work, or at a local community site. The greatest appeal of distance learning is that you can participate in courses—often at times convenient to you—without having to leave home or a job to go to campus. Perhaps you live in a rural area, or are caring for young children. Or you have a full-time job but need to get an advanced degree. Or you need additional education to enter a new career field. Or you want to get a two-year degree now and may transfer to a four-year program later. Maybe you are physically disabled and would find it hard to get to a campus.

Distance learning is not for everyone. But some people find distance learning the perfect way to fit an educational pursuit into their busy lives. Once you understand all your options, you can decide if distance learning is for you.

DISTANCE LEARNING: HOW QUICKLY IT CHANGES

Distance learning is not a new concept. Today's distance learning programs are descendants of the correspondence courses that were first offered early in the twentieth century and are still available today. Correspondence courses rely on written course materials sent through the mail, whereas most distance education courses now use technology to deliver some or all of the course materials and provide instruction.

The technologies used in distance learning have evolved rapidly. In the first half of the twentieth century, radio was used to deliver education at a distance, and in the 1950s, local educational television stations developed. The Public Broadcasting Service's telecourses were seen nationwide from the 1960s to the 1980s. At that point, interactive video technologies began to gain popularity. Telecourses and video are still widely used, but in the 1990s, computer and multimedia technologies became the most prevalent telecommunications media used in distance learning.

Distance learning has seen enormous growth in the last decade. According to the U. S. Department of Education, about one third of higher education institutions offered distance learning courses in 1995. By the 2000–2001 academic year that was up to 56 percent. These same surveys indicate that public institutions are more likely than private to offer distance learning. In 2001, about 90 percent of all public two-year and four-year institutions had distance learning courses or programs.

TECHNOLOGY-SUPPORTED LEARNING

The opportunities made available by technology are changing not only distance learning, but learning on campus as well. In fact, technology-supported learning is blurring the distinction between distance learning and any learning that relies on technological media. Many on-campus students take some courses in a classroom setting and others via the Internet. And there are many examples of a "blended" approach, in which an on-campus course includes an online component.

In today's technology-based environment, you may find that education is becoming more learner centered than teacher centered. This learner-centered approach focuses on creating an environment in which you, as learner, can be actively involved in your learning instead of passively absorbing information conveyed by the instructor.

TECHNOLOGIES USED IN DISTANCE LEARNING

Almost all distance learning technologies are based on one or a combination of just three media: computer, telephone, and video.

COMPUTER

- **Internet-based education** has become the most dominant form of distance education. According to the U. S. Department of Education study *A Profile of Participation in Distance Education: 1999–2000*, about 60 percent of undergraduate and 67 percent of graduate students did so via the Internet. Internet-based education requires a student to have a computer connected to the Internet, which links computers all over the world. A variety of tools are then available:
  - The World Wide Web is like having the largest library and entertainment center in the world at your fingertips.
  - Email enables instructors and students to communicate quickly across time and distance by typing messages to each other.
- A variety of applications increase the interactivity of the Web to create collaborative virtual work spaces for student–student and student–instructor interactions. These applications make it possible for you to work cooperatively on projects with other students, no matter how far apart you are:
  - Streaming audio lets Web users hear a sound file while they view a picture of the person speaking when the file was made. Streaming video allows users to view moving images over the Internet.
  - Computer conferencing can be set up either as real-time "chat" spaces so that participants can interact at the same time or as systems that do not require participants to be present at the same time.

- **Stand-alone computer-based programs** deliver self-paced instruction via CD-ROM, diskette, or connection to a local area or wide area network.

Despite the dominance of the Internet, it is important to remember that both telephone and video technologies are still quite commonly used to provide distance education. The same study mentioned previously found that in 1999–2000, about 37 percent of undergraduate students who participated in distance education did so via live, interactive TV or audio, and 39 percent participated using prerecorded TV or audio.

TELEPHONE

- **Audioconferencing** enables instructors and students at multiple sites to communicate with each other via telephone.
- **Audiographics** is a form of teleconferencing that uses both an audio and a data connection. Students can speak with the instructor and students at other sites and, via computer, can view graphics and pictures developed by the instructor. Students may also be able to use an electronic pen and tablet to mark on the visuals, as on a board in a regular classroom.
- **Fax** allows students and faculty to send materials electronically or on paper over phone lines.

VIDEO

- **Telecourses** are taped or live television programs carried by broadcast or cable television stations. A study guide for each course provides directions and assignments to students.
- **Videotapes** are videos recorded during a class period or tapes reproduced especially for a distance learning class. Students can view them at their convenience via TV and video cassette recorder (VCR) at home.
- **One-way video** transmits video signals live in one direction: from the instructor to learners. (The basic technology can be Instructional Fixed Television Service [IFTS], cable or satellite.) Students can receive the video transmission in a classroom or through a desktop videoconferencing unit. During the class period, off-site students can communicate with the instructor over the phone or through a return key.

- **Interactive video** systems (two or more locations) equip each location with cameras, monitors, and microphones, enabling those at the origination site and those in off-site classrooms to see and hear each other.

What you are almost certain to find is that courses may include a blend of approaches and technologies, with each being used as the instructor chooses, to enhance students' learning experiences. And always, just over the horizon is a new technology or software package with the potential to change the face of distance learning in yet another way—and possibly to improve learning as well.

WHICH TECHNOLOGY IS BEST?

The technologies used in distance learning are enablers. They are only tools, not the real point of distance learning. What really matters is how engaged you are in your learning experiences. The more involved and active you are, the more you will learn.

No single technology is best for distance learning. The technology that is most appropriate for one course or one student may be totally unsuitable for another. The best distance learning experiences, in fact, may be those that combine a variety of technologies for different purposes. For example, you may find that a course offered via two-way video also includes an email component to encourage students' interaction outside class with each other and the instructor.

Your own situation gives you some clues about what technological media (and therefore what specific courses) are available to you. If a course is offered via videotape, for example, and you don't have access to a VCR, there's no point in enrolling in that course. Likewise, if you don't have access to a computer, you can't enroll in an online course.

SYNCHRONOUS VERSUS ASYNCHRONOUS COMMUNICATION: A CRUCIAL DIFFERENCE

There are two basic ways of thinking about distance learning. The terms *synchronous communication* and *asynchronous communication* explain the essential differences by defining the extent to which instruction is bounded by time.

1. **Synchronous communication** is communication in which all parties participate at the same time. Synchronous communication in distance learning emphasizes a simultaneous group learning experience. Teachers and students communicate in "real time," usually via interactive audio- or videoconferencing from a classroom to one or more remote classrooms. If you take a course that uses synchronous communication, you must attend at a specified time and in a specified place.

   Synchronous communication may be thought of as an extended classroom—even if the "classroom" is your bedroom computer workstation. Technologies used for synchronous delivery include interactive audio and video; audiographics; and some GroupWare applications, such as online "chat rooms," in which students communicate via the computer at the same time but from different places.

2. **Asynchronous communication** is communication in which parties participate at different times. Asynchronous communication offers a choice of where and, above all, *when* you will access learning. In a class using asynchronous communication, you can learn any time and any place you choose. Internet-based courses belong in this category, as do videotapes, email, listservs, and correspondence courses. In an asynchronous course, the instructor usually posts on the Internet the lesson materials and assignments for the course. You may read or view these materials at your own convenience. After you have completed the assigned activities, you send your completed work (via computer, fax, or regular mail) to the instructor for evaluation.

   Since you study and do the course work on your own time, wherever it is convenient, asynchronous classes may seem to emphasize only individual learning. However, asynchronous learning can also be a group experience. In this type of learning, the interactions with your instructor and fellow students don't take place in "real time," that is, simultaneously. Instead, each of you works at your own pace, contributing to a group discussion by posting comments on the computer or even by leaving each other voice mail messages.

You'll find as many variations among distance learning classes as you've no doubt experienced among regular classrooms. This makes it hard to generalize. But the two examples presented here offer at least a general idea of what it might be like for you to take part in two common versions of distance learning classes.

Synchronous Communication: An Extended Classroom

Where and when.　You attend class sessions at a specific time and place—often three times a week, but at least once a week. The instructor is located—along with the "on-site students"—in a classroom on campus. You are likely to be in one of several groups gathered at various off-campus sites, such as public libraries, community colleges, cooperative extension offices, or regional learning centers near where you live or work. Often videotapes of televised classes are available for student use and review later.

The experience.　The "feel" of the class depends partly on the technology used. There's an obvious difference, of course, between the experience of a class delivered via audio (where you can only hear each other) and one that uses two-way video (where you can also see each other). But in all cases, you and the other off-site students will be able to participate in the class as it is taking place—in real time.

In a class using two-way video, the sound and picture on the video screen may or may not, depending on the exact technology used, be as smoothly coordinated as in a regular broadcast TV show. Everyone's movements may look a bit jerky, and there might be a brief delay between the sound of a speaker's voice and the speaker's picture. However, you'll be able to see and hear the on-site students and the teacher and they, in turn, will see and hear you. If a technical problem crops up during the class, a local technician will usually be available to fix it.

Tests.　Classes taught via distance learning technologies face a special problem when it comes to exam time. To be fair to everyone in the course, your instructor must make sure that students taking the test are actually enrolled. One way to ensure this is to require everyone to take exams on-campus. However, some students may deem this unfair, or it may be impractical, especially if the students in the course are widely dispersed. As an alternative, colleges often appoint off-site proctors to check the identity of students. And in two-way video classes, the instructor can see students in the remote classroom whenever the camera pans the room. Some faculty rely on this method of ensuring exam integrity, whereas others feel more comfortable having exam proctors at each off-site location.

Faculty–student interaction outside the course.　As a distance learner, you may not be able to talk with your instructor in person during his or her office hours. This does not mean that the lines of communication are cut off between class periods. Your instructor will make clear on the course syllabus some specific times and ways for you to ask questions and contact him or her outside class. For example, if you have access to email, you may be able to contact your instructor easily through that means, or your instructor may give you a phone number (sometimes toll-free) or a fax number. So there's no need to worry—even from a distance, help from your instructor should always be there when you need it.

Student interaction outside the course.   Students who take a class together in a local community often form close learning groups. You might meet with a group for coffee to study together, or you might exchange phone numbers. So if you miss a class session and need to catch up on assignments, you'll be able to contact someone from your class who can help bring you up to speed. The instructor may, in addition, set up threaded listservs or chat rooms to enable you and the students at all sites to communicate with each other.

Asynchronous Communication: As It Suits You

The most important feature of an asynchronous course is that you can take it wherever and whenever it suits you. Although the following description is of an online course, remember that asynchronous courses may be offered via precorded videotape or audiotape, or even correspondence.

Where and when.   Anywhere, anytime. The instructor puts learning materials on the Internet, and you and other students may access these materials at any time before the assignment is due. You can study at home, at your workplace, or in a hotel room while you're traveling on business—wherever it's convenient.

You may be able to register online for a course or program, order books, or complete applications for financial aid. Some online courses may offer scheduled synchronous possibilities, such as chat rooms, where a teacher and students arrange to be online at the same time.

The experience.   The materials for the class probably will be organized in electronic folders according to date. The materials can be designed for everyone in the class or personalized for individual students. Information can be linked to additional resources on the Web. Most online courses emphasize collaboration and communication, often using

Web-based message systems to connect students with each other and the instructor.

It might seem that studying online would make you feel isolated from the rest of the class and the instructor. However, students report that, on the contrary, they feel *more* a part of the class than they did in a traditional classroom. People often find that they are drawn into the subject matter of a class, because of the online discussions they have with their peers and instructor.

Tests.   Many online courses are designed so that there are no conventional "tests." Instead, instructors rely on a series of writing assignments, open-book exams, and/or problem-solving assignments to gauge a student's progress through a course. The issue of exam integrity is a difficult one when everyone is working on a computer at home. A number of online security systems have been developed, which require every user to log on with a user name and a password, and software to detect plagiarism is also available. However, even these systems cannot ensure that the only person in the room is the enrolled student. Therefore, some online courses are run on the honor system, and others actually encourage collaborative work among groups of students who are evaluated together.

Faculty–student interaction outside the course.   Online classes offer many ways for students and instructors to communicate. Since every student in the class obviously has access to a computer and the Internet, instructors can set up a variety of computer-based methods for communication. In addition to regular email, these may include online discussions.

Student interaction outside the course.   In many online classes, the instructor encourages students to work together on projects even though they live far apart from each other and have different schedules. Interactive software can make this kind of collaborative effort possible, and online chat rooms facilitate discussions among class members. In other classes, students may work more independently, relying on email to communicate with each other.

WHO ARE DISTANCE LEARNERS?

Most distance learners are over 25 years old, have a job, and have previously completed some education beyond high school. About 60 percent are women. Distance learners are people who, because of time, place, or other constraints, choose not to pursue their educational goals in a traditional on-campus setting.

Distance learners have many different backgrounds and educational goals. They include adults returning to college, first-time students, midcareer professionals seeking continuing education, workers obtaining a credential to make a job change possible, students with physical and learning disabilities, and geographically isolated students. Here are a few examples:

Sarah L. lives in Chicago, where she works full-time as a teller at a large bank downtown. For the last three years, she has been taking classes to complete her bachelor's degree in accounting, so she can move into the accounting department at the bank. Until she began taking videotaped courses, her progress in completing her degree had been slow. Sarah is a divorced mother with two children—ages three and six—and balancing work, child care, and school made it difficult to attend even a single course each semester at any of the many colleges in Chicago. The flexibility of videotaped courses has made it possible for her to finish 12 credit hours in the last year. Sarah watches the preproduced video lectures and does her assignments at home in the evening after her children are in bed and on alternate weekends when they are visiting their father. She interacts with her professor and other students using a sophisticated voice mail system.

Lauren and Robert F. are both orthopedic surgeons at a large hospital in Rhode Island. They have worked together at this hospital for the last 16 years. For most of that time, they have struggled to fit required continuing education courses into their demanding schedules, swapping evenings with the children and nights on call to drive to seminars and classes. Last year, Lauren attended a lecture about the benefits of online learning and tried her first course, which was offered by a top medical school. "In a profession where an average of 20 continuing education courses are required every two years, online learning really makes sense," Lauren says. Robert agrees: "The Web is the perfect medium for the dynamic field of medicine."

Michael J. needs a bachelor's degree to advance profession-
ally, but he lives in a small town in eastern Oregon, quite distant from the nearest higher-education institution offering
four-year degrees. After a bit of investigating, he finds that
Eastern Oregon University offers an External Degree in Liberal Studies at regional centers throughout the eastern portion
of the state. Michael enrolls in the program, which uses a
satellite-based video network to deliver courses at a center
near his home. He is pleased with the quality of the courses he
has taken and also with the one-to-one help he has received
from the regional center's coordinator, who has helped him
plan his program, semester by semester, to completion.
Michael now has only three more courses to finish before receiving his degree.

Paul R. lives in Milan, Italy, where his wife, Emma, is completing her active duty in the military. Paul is a freelance pho-
tographer and is used to traveling. He has always liked
learning, but Emma's career has made it difficult for him to enroll in traditional university courses. In the past two years, she
has been assigned to new posts three times. The nearest university hasn't always offered the courses Paul wants to take in
English, so he considered taking courses online. Initially, Paul
was worried, because he doesn't know a lot about computers,
but he found that the courses were designed for new users. He
took his first online course when he and Emma lived in Frank-
furt, Germany, and continues to take a course each semester.
For Paul, online courses are fun. In addition, he has found that
they give him a link to the United States and provide him with
a real, if virtual, community, something that isn't always easy
to find abroad.

Characteristics of Successful Distance Learners

Those who succeed as distance learners

- are highly motivated.
- are independent.
- are active learners.
- have good organizational and time management skills.
- have the discipline to study without external reminders.
- can adapt to new learning environments.

These may sound like the qualities needed to succeed in any learning environment—and, indeed, they are. But the distance learning context puts special pressures on learners to be independent and self-disciplined.

If you are considering distance learning, it may be partly because you have multiple responsibilities. The reality that you are balancing an already busy life means that you, like other distance learners, need to have strong motivation and the ability to structure your world to allow you the time to study. *The fact is that you are likely to find that distance learning is more, not less, demanding than learning through traditional means.*

Successful distance learners develop their own support systems, either through electronic gatherings or in person. Chapter 6 offers some specific suggestions to help you succeed in a distance learning environment.

EARNING A DEGREE

Is it possible to earn an entire degree without setting foot on a campus? Yes, it certainly is. Chapter 2 provides detailed information about finding an appropriate distance education program through which you can earn a degree.

Undergraduate degrees. Two-year associate degrees are the fastest growing segment of distance learning. Public Broadcasting Service's *Going the Distance* program, offered by a consortium of public television stations and community colleges nationwide, makes available a complete associate degree for adults who could not otherwise obtain a degree. A number of colleges are offering online associate degrees—either alone or in consortia formed with other colleges in their state.

It is also easy to find four-year bachelor's degree programs (B.S. or B.A.) offered at a distance by higher education institutions. Business, liberal arts, and computer science fields are the four-year degrees most often offered via distance learning technologies. There are also several bachelor's degree completion programs, which enable students with associate degrees to complete the remaining requirements for a bachelor's at a distance.

There are a variety of ways you can earn an undergraduate degree as a distance learner:

1. **Complete a full degree program from a single institution.** Several years ago, most colleges and universities offered only a smattering of individual courses to students at a distance, but a large number of institutions—including top-ranked colleges and universities—now offer full degree programs via technology. As a result, you are likely to be able to find a complete program in the field in which you are interested. It may even be offered at a distance by an institution you have always dreamed of attending.

2. **Accumulate credits from several institutions.** Another way you can achieve a degree from a distance is to accumulate courses and credits from more than one college or university. However, before embarking on this route, be sure that the courses and credits you plan to earn from one institution will be accepted toward a degree that you hope to receive from another. Transferring credits is like doing a picture puzzle: to fit, the pieces must be of the same picture.

3. **Prove your competency.** It is also sometimes possible to get a degree via distance learning by enrolling in an institution that bases credentials on proven competencies rather than on earned credit hours. Traditionally, higher-education institutions have awarded degrees when a student has accumulated a certain number of credit hours in required subjects. However, this new model is based on independent verification of a learner's competency. Under this system, you, as a student, might obtain formal recognition for your prior learning or prove your competency through assessments, and then enroll in only the courses you need to complete a degree program.

Even some conventional institutions, which rely on the course credit system rather than demonstrated competencies, will let you earn credits by "testing out" of a particular course by demonstrating your competency.

Postgraduate degrees. It is also possible to earn advanced degrees from a distance. Master's degrees are available in a number of fields, but especially in business, education, nursing, engineering, and computer science. Some of these programs may require at least a short period of on-campus attendance. Ph.D. and professional programs, such as medicine or law, almost always require some time on campus.

Is a Degree Earned via Technology Equal to One Earned on Campus?

You may be skeptical that a degree earned via technology at a distance will be valued as highly as one earned through on-campus study. You may wonder whether such a degree might be judged inferior when you seek a job or apply to graduate school. The answer to this understandable concern is that both employers and graduate schools now generally consider degrees earned via technology at a distance equivalent to those earned on campus. Most colleges and universities are genuinely committed to ensuring that distance degrees represent the same quality as traditional degree programs. Indeed, at some institutions, your transcript will look identical to one received through on-campus study.

In the past, there was certainly prejudice against a degree earned from a distance rather than in the traditional way. However, these attitudes are rapidly changing as colleges and universities diligently work to create excellent distance learning programs—and as former distance learners demonstrate their worth in the workplace and in top-notch graduate schools.

What About Taking Just a Few Courses?

Not a bad idea. Thousands of courses are available, both for credit and for noncredit. If you are just beginning to consider pursuing a degree via distance learning, you might wish to enroll in a course or two to see how you like distance learning, whether it fits your life and your learning style. Many people are taking distance learning courses for personal enrichment or just for fun. Noncredit courses may appeal to you for these reasons.

Doctors, nurses, teachers, and those in some other professional fields must take a certain number of hours in continuing education each year. They earn Continuing Education Units (CEUs) this way. Distance learning is becoming increasingly popular as a way to earn CEUs. If you plan to pursue required continuing education through distance education, however, be sure to find out if credits from the program you are considering will be accepted.

Even if you are already enrolled in a campus-based degree program, there are many reasons you might wish to enroll in a few courses at a distance. Here are some of them:

- You need a specific course to graduate, but all on-campus sections are full or not offered at a convenient time.
- You wish to take a course in an area of interest from a noted professor who teaches via distance learning.
- You are interested in a course that isn't offered at your college or university.
- You are in a hurry to graduate or wish to have some free time over the summer.

In short, there are many opportunities for taking a particular course and many valid reasons for doing so.

Will Another College Accept Distance Education Credits?

Sometimes, but you should check in advance. Individual institutions determine the transferability of credits. It may depend on factors such as whether the institution where you took the credits was accredited and whether the course itself was considered academic in nature. If you are enrolled in a degree program at one college and would like to transfer credit hours earned at a distance from another institution, be sure to find out if those courses will fulfill your "home" institution's requirements.

Some institutions have established formal relationships with other colleges; these colleges have mutually agreed to accept each other's courses. In other cases, a two-year college may have developed what are called *articulation agreements*, or guaranteed transfer, with four-year institutions in the state. Within some state university systems, credits are transferable between institutions.

THE QUALITY QUESTION

The question of distance learning's quality is bound to be important to you. An inferior education will prove fruitless, no matter what your goals. However, distance learning does match up to traditional classroom approaches.

"No significant difference." This phrase sums up the result of hundreds of research studies on whether students studying at a distance perform as well as their counterparts in traditional classrooms. The research findings indicate that students studying at a distance do as well as on-site students on exams and other measures of achievement. They also suggest that having an instructor in the classroom is no more effective than providing instruction at a distance using technology.

IS DISTANCE LEARNING FOR YOU?

By now, you should have a sense of the types of distance learning and how distance learning can meet various student interests and needs. You may be close to taking the plunge into the world of distance learning.

But before you do, consider carefully *what kind of learner* you are and what your *educational* and *professional goals* are. Are you

- serious, self-motivated, and disciplined?
- comfortable with the idea of learning via technology?
- persistent and resourceful in solving problems?

Think again about your goals. Here are some questions to help you consider your own needs:

- What is my educational goal? Do I need to develop some specific skills in the shortest time possible? Do I need a credit course that I can put on my transcript? Do I want to begin a complete degree program? What do I really want?
- Do I have a timetable or a specific date by which I need to complete this education?
- Do I want to go to school part-time or full-time?
- Will I be working at the same time? Part-time or full-time? Will my employer reimburse my tuition costs?

- Can I go to a campus or a local learning center (for several meetings in a semester or to access a computer lab), or must the entire educational experience be offered at a distance?

- How do I feel about various educational delivery methods? Would I be willing to interact over a computer, watch videotapes, or listen to audiotapes?

- Do I have a computer or access to one? Am I willing to buy a computer? Do I have adequate computer competency skills? (For a discussion of technology requirements, see Chapter 3.)

- How much time can I commit to my course work? When can I do it? Will I have some time at work? Will I find time late at night or early in the morning at home?

- Is cost an important consideration? How much can I afford to spend each month or each semester for tuition and other charges? Do I need to look for an institution that will provide financial assistance?

This list is by no means comprehensive. It's a starting point. *You* must determine your needs. Then you must see if available distance learning opportunities can meet them.

You may also wish to consider your personal learning preference to discover more about how you learn best. (You will learn more about these learning preferences in Chapter 6.) Some of us learn best through listening, others through active participation, and still others by reading. Most people use a combination of learning styles. Ask your nearest college administrator to provide a learning-style test so you can determine what kind of learner you are. If the college doesn't provide such testing, ask the administrator to refer you to someone who does.

CAUTION: LONG-TERM PLANNING AHEAD

If after considering your goals and commitments you decide that distance learning might meet your needs, you still have a great deal of investigating to do. Enrolling in a distance learning program means investing a lot of your time and money, especially if you intend to earn a degree. It is therefore important to take the time to identify your needs clearly and to find a course of study and reliable institution to help you meet those needs (see Chapter 2).

BEWARE OF "DIPLOMA MILLS"

Although many excellent institutions offer high-quality distance learning programs, there are a few unscrupulous providers in the business as well. Some "diploma mills" churn out diplomas without caring whether they are really earned or not. As long as someone is willing to pay, these "institutions" are willing to grant certification.

The most important way to protect yourself and be sure that you are enrolling in a quality program is to ask the following question: "Is a reputable institution offering this course or program?" Remember that it is easy to put the words *College* or *University* into the title of a business. These terms, suggesting institutional legitimacy, may mean nothing at all.

This information is just an early warning signal. Chapter 2 addresses the subject of quality, including accreditation, and gives some specific questions you should ask of any institution from which you are considering taking courses.

SUMMARY: YOU'RE ON YOUR WAY

In this chapter, you've learned the basics about distance learning. You've been introduced to some distance learners and the reasons they chose to pursue their educational goals via distance learning. You now know that you must examine your own goals carefully and take stock of whether you believe you have the personal qualities you will need to succeed in this new environment. Hopefully, you've also acquired a real sense of what it would be like to enroll in a course or program delivered at a distance, and you have found answers to any questions you might have had about whether distance learning can match the quality of a traditional approach.

In short, this chapter has shown you how distance learning can offer a route along the information highway toward the education you want. Do you want to travel further? If so, the following chapters are your guide for the rest of the way.

 www.DLGuide.info
Visit this website for additional information and activities.

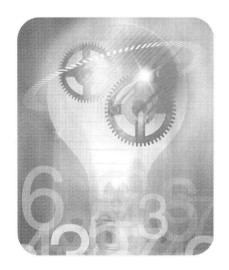

CHAPTER 2

CHOOSING A DISTANCE EDUCATION PROVIDER

Asking the Right Questions

In this chapter you will

- learn various ways to identify providers of distance education
- become familiar with the academic and student service issues important to your success as a distance learner
- be given a list of questions to ask of each potential distance learning provider

LOCATING DISTANCE EDUCATION PROVIDERS AND PROGRAMS

Once you have determined your personal learning or professional development needs, it is time to look for the provider that comes closest to meeting them. Let's begin by determining which institutions to approach first.

The past few years have seen remarkable growth in the number of institutions offering distance learning options. In the previous chapter, we mentioned the U. S. Department of Education studies that track this growth. From 1995 to 1997 the percentage of *all* higher education institutions offering distance learning went from 33 to 44. By 2001, about 90 percent of all public institutions had distance learning courses or programs. In addition, almost every state has created a virtual university to serve students who want or need distance learning opportunities. These range from institutions that offer only a few courses, such as faculty teaching at remote sites, a few courses offered by interactive television, and computer-based courses offered over the Internet, to institutions that offer one or more complete degrees at a distance. How should you go about sorting them out to find the one that is the best match for you?

PROVIDERS CLOSE TO HOME

There are two reasons that you should start by considering the public institutions that are geographically close to you: (1) if a nearby institution offers what you want through distance learning, you are likely to find better support services, and (2) the in-state tuition is likely to be less expensive. If there is no program close to your home, look at other public institutions within your state. Again, the services are likely to be more available, and you will be paying in-state tuition.

Next, consider the private institutions in your state. Although they are likely to be more expensive, the difference in cost for distance learners may not be as much as you might expect.

Each state has an education office that is responsible for collecting and disseminating information about higher education in that state. The office for your state should be listed in your local phone book. In addition, all states have a website. For example, you could find information about higher education in Maine by going to **www.maine.gov** and then clicking on higher education. Another way to find your state's higher education office is to visit **www.sheeo.org** and click on Higher Ed Links.

REGIONAL AND NATIONAL PROVIDERS

A third option for finding a distance education provider is to look regionally and nationally. Two types of organizations should have information about these distance learning opportunities. One is the regional accrediting association in a multistate area (there are eight in the United States), such as the New England Association of Schools and Colleges, Inc. The second is a regional higher education association, such as the Western Interstate Commission for Higher Education (**www.wiche.edu**) or the Southern Regional Education Board (**www.sreb.org**).

The regional accrediting associations will be able to provide you with information about which of the distance education institutions are accredited, and the regional higher education associations will be able to provide a variety of information about those institutions. We have provided contact information on our website.

USING PRINT AND ELECTRONIC SOURCES TO FIND A PROVIDER

A final way to find a provider is to search for the course or program using one of the several print and electronic sources for finding information about distance education opportunities.

There are two important reference books that provide information about institutions offering distance learning. Peterson's *Guide to Distance Learning Programs 2003* (Princeton, NJ: Peterson's, 2003) lists the courses and programs of more than 1,100 accredited distance learning institutions in the United States and Canada. This book is designed to be updated every year or two since the number of institutions entering the distance education marketplace is expanding rapidly each year. For example, the 1998 edition listed only 800 distance learning programs. Offerings are listed by institutions that offer (1) degree and certificate programs and (2) individual courses. There is also an index of institutions by state and Canadian province that offer distance learning. For each institution there is a detailed profile that describes the institution, the course delivery sites (e.g., home, high schools, workplace), media used (e.g., television, radio, email), services provided (e.g., library, computer, email, advising, career counseling), credit-earning options, typical costs, registration procedures, and contact information at the institution.

Bears' Guide to Earning Degrees by Distance Learning (15th ed.), by John and Mariah Bear, details information on more than 2,500 schools. It covers all degree levels and provides tips on how to obtain credit for life experiences. The Bears also have published a variety of other reference books on distance learning, including *College Degrees by Mail and Internet*. Visit **www.degree.net** for additional books and information.

A good electronic information source is the website for the National Center for Education Statistics (**http://nces.ed.gov/ipeds/cool/ indix.asp**), which provides state-by-state information on accredited higher education institutions. This site links you to more than 7,000 colleges and universities in the United States. Included on this site is IPEDS College Opportunities On-line (COOL), a search function that can find a college based on its location, program, or degree offerings.

The Southern Regional Education Board has developed a new online service termed a regional *learning network* (**www.electroniccampus.org**). It helps distance education students enroll in Web-based courses and also receive academic support. The program, called Ways in Mentor (**www.waysin.org**), allows students to apply to multiple colleges online and keeps centralized records listing which courses students have completed.

As you complete the task of finding courses or programs that fit your needs, you should have identified several potential provider institutions. The next step is to contact each institution to determine the services it provides for distant students. It is in the area of support services that you are likely to find the greatest differences among institutions.

Finally, a word of caution: there are fake institutions that prey on the unwary. To help you steer clear of these unscrupulous institutions, the *Bears' Guide* maintains updated information on diploma mills as well as more suggestions on how to evaluate colleges.

Questions to Ask Distance Education Providers

Most of our understanding of higher education institutions is based on previous experiences on a college campus, where a wide range of academic and student services are offered through various offices. For the distance learner, however, these services have to be provided by the institution in a different fashion. There is great variation in the way that institutions have addressed these distance learning support issues.

The next step in choosing a provider is comparing the range of services that each institution offers to distance education students. Students often assume that an institution offering courses or programs at a distance will also provide all of the essential services at a distance. In fact, this is far from true. Many institutions have found it easier to put courses and degrees on the Web than to reorganize campus services that are essential for distance learners.

The importance of institutional services for you as a distance learner cannot be overemphasized. To be blunt, if the institution has not organized services to support you at a distance, you are likely to spend an enormous amount of time trying to connect to an office or individual at the institution, trying to navigate its various campus-based processes (e.g., admissions, registration, financial aid, advising, computer connections, library support), and trying to handle the logistics of sending and securing academic materials. If the services are not in place, problems will persist throughout your program. To avoid the frustration of enrolling in an institution that is not organized to serve you, be careful to obtain answers to each of the questions we have listed on the following pages. A small amount of your time spent researching the services of institutions will have a terrific payoff as you move smoothly through your program.

There are a number of questions to ask each institution. Although this may appear tedious, you will find that the answer to each question is basically "yes" or "no." To make this part of your research easier, we have included on our companion website a worksheet that you can print and use to record the responses of each institution to the questions outlined in the following sections. This form will make comparing responses among institutions much easier. Remember that you are looking for the institution that has the maximum number of "yes" answers.

General Issues

A website. An institution involved in distance learning usually will have a first-rate website describing the programs and services it offers at a distance. If the institution has been serving students at a distance for more than a year or two, it is likely to have a Web section for "Frequently Asked Questions (FAQs)."

1 *Does the institution have a website with information about distance learning offerings and services?*

Phone access.   Being a distance learning student means that you are physically removed from the traditional opportunities for face-to-face communication with instructors and campus offices, but it should not mean that you are a "lonely" or "isolated" learner. It is important to ensure that you replace in-person meetings with other forms of communication. For some purposes, the telephone will be your most effective and convenient means of communication. If the institution is in your local calling area, phone access will be easy. However, if it is a toll call, you need to determine who is going to be paying the long distance charges. If you are the one who will have to pay for these calls, you might avoid making them in order to save money.

2 *Is the institution in your local calling area?*

3 *If your answer to question 2 is "no," does the institution have a toll-free number for distance learners that will allow you to connect with faculty and the various campus offices?*

An orientation handbook for distance learners.   It is enormously helpful if the institution has thought through all of the issues and topics of interest to distance learners and put together relevant policies and procedures in a single document. This will save you time in evaluating the institution's commitment to distance learners.

4 *Does the institution have an orientation handbook for distance learners?*

Orientation for distance students.   Once you have decided to enroll at an institution, you might find it helpful to participate in an orientation for distance students. Such an orientation would normally be offered at a distance. An orientation may provide tips on a variety of ways to make learning at a distance easier. Many orientations feature faculty and current students who have special insight into successful distance learning strategies. If the institution you are considering has an orientation program, be sure to take advantage of it.

5 *Does the institution have an orientation for distance learners?*

A single point of contact. One of the major frustrations of distance learners is not being able to contact the appropriate person or office on a campus to answer a question, to process paperwork, or to solve a problem. Those institutions that are designed to serve the distance learner normally will have a single point of contact, such as an Office of Distance (or Distributed) Learning.

6 *Does the institution have a designated distance education office?*

7 *If so, does this office provide "one-stop" services in the areas of admissions? registration? financial aid applications?*

A contact person. You will need a contact person at the institution to serve as your advisor and advocate. You will have numerous process questions related to your program, so it is important to have the same person on campus to call on each time to answer your questions.

8 *Will you be assigned an advisor who will assist you in weaving your way through the institutional requirements and processes?*

Accreditation. Institutions that have achieved regional and professional accreditation have met a set of rigorous educational standards. (A listing of all of the regional accrediting associations is provided on our website.) Accredited institutions are recognized by the U. S. Department of Education and approved to award federal financial aid. In addition, other accredited institutions usually accept their credits in transfer. In selecting your program, all things being equal, your top priority should be an accredited institution.

9 *Is the institution regionally accredited?*

10 *Is the institution accredited by some other federally recognized agency?*

Furthermore, many programs lead to some sort of state or national certification and/or examination (e.g., a nursing degree). You need to be sure that the institution has state or professional approval to offer a degree for which you will have to take a professional examination or seek state licensure.

11 *Does a professional accrediting association accredit the program in which you are interested?*

12 *If so, has that professional association approved the program to be offered at a distance?*

13 *Does the program in which you are interested need to be certified by the state?*

14 *Upon graduation, will you be able to take the state examination for certification?*

Transfer credit. You may want to use credits that you have accumulated at a previous institution in the program you have now selected. It is therefore important to make sure that all credits earned elsewhere are transferred before you begin the program.

15 *Will the institution accept credits that you have earned previously?*

16 *If so, how many?*

Transcript and diploma. You need to make sure that the transcript and the diploma that you receive from the institution are the same as you would receive if you took the program totally on campus. You do not want a transcript or diploma that identifies your courses or program as different from that on campus, in order to ensure that a future employer or others will not interpret the degree as second class.

17 *Will my transcript and diploma look the same as if I had taken the courses on campus?*

Academic Issues

Academic advisor. You will have a number of questions about the program in which you plan to enroll, so make sure you have an academic advisor, usually a faculty member in the program, before enrolling. This could be the same person as the previously mentioned "Contact Person." Having one person with whom you can raise questions and discuss program issues is very important.

18 *Will you be assigned an academic advisor?*

19 *Will the advisor be assigned before you enroll to help you choose courses?*

Percentage of the program at a distance. At the outset, you need to know how much of the program in which you are enrolling is available fully at a distance. If there are any courses, portions of courses, laboratories, discussions, examinations, or other components of the program that will require you to go to the campus or another location, you need to know this in advance. You should inquire about prerequisite courses and any general education requirements that may precede your work in the major. When you inquire about the percentage of the program offered at a distance, make sure that the institution understands that you are asking about *every* requirement of the program including internships and externships. Finally, you also need to know well in advance if any location-specific requirements are scheduled so that you can fit them into your own calendar.

20 *Is 100 percent of the program offered at a distance?*

21 *If not, what percentage of the program is available at a distance?*

Residency requirement. The vast majority of higher education institutions have requirements about the number of credits you must take on the campus, or at an approved off-campus location, in order to complete graduation. This requirement ranges from one-quarter to one-half of the credits needed to graduate. If the institution counts for residency all courses offered by the institution, regardless of where the student is located, then the distance student can meet the requirement. If the requirement specifies some amount of time on campus, this may be a major barrier to your timely completion of the program.

An institution that has recently begun offering degrees at a distance may not have revised all of its own internal campus policies to take into account the realities of distance learners. You must resolve this issue before you enroll in a program. If the program does not have a waiver of the residency requirement for distance students, you need to consider whether you can fit travel to a campus or another site into your schedule.

22 *Does the institution have a residency requirement?*

23 *If so, can a distance student fulfill the requirement at a distance?*

Sequencing of courses. Most degree programs do not offer all of their courses each semester. Courses in a major are often alternated between fall and spring semesters and, usually, they are offered only once a year.

Some institutions are admitting a "cohort" of students who begin a program as a group and move through it, usually part-time, taking two courses per semester, until they finish together in two to four years. The advantage of the "cohort" system (beyond being able to go through a program with the same group of students, even if virtually) is that the institution guarantees a sequencing of courses and you know which courses you will be taking each semester of the program. This is very important because the sequencing plan has accounted for prerequisites and a logical progression through the program.

You need to be sure that the institution has thought through the sequencing so that all of the courses you need will be offered in the necessary period for you to complete your degree. If a course you need isn't going to be offered during the semester you need it, find out if you will be allowed to take the course from some other institution and have it accepted in transfer.

24 *Does the institution have a logical sequencing of courses?*

25 *Does the institution guarantee that the courses will be offered in the sequence listed?*

Substituting courses from other institutions.   Although you may never need to exercise this option, it is useful to know if you can take a course from another institution and substitute it for one in your program. For example, if you or a family member were ill for a time, or your job responsibilities changed, you might have to withdraw from a course that wouldn't be offered for another year. Having the option of being able to take the course elsewhere in the summer or a subsequent semester would allow you to progress toward your degree on schedule.

26 *Does the institution allow courses to be substituted from other institutions?*

27 *If so, is there a limit?*

Placement or admissions testing.   If there are any tests that you must take before admission (e.g., the Scholastic Aptitude Test or Graduate Record Exam), you should know about them and where they are offered. You should also know if you are required to take any placement examinations (e.g., math or a foreign language). Moreover, you should know if your performance on these tests could affect whether you can take your entire program at a distance.

28 *Are there any required examinations that you must take before enrollment?*

29 *If so, are they offered at a distance?*

30 *Could your performance on any examination influence whether you can take your entire program at a distance?*

Library access. Libraries are rapidly moving toward providing information and resources electronically. You will be able to complete an enormous amount of research over the Web. However, actually securing library resources can often be one of the most difficult problems for distance learners. If you live in a rural area that does not have a college or university library nearby, you need to consider how your library needs will be met. A reasonable expectation is that the distance learning institution will have made some special provisions for making library materials available to distance learners, including interlibrary loan, 48-hour delivery, or faxing services. At the very least, it is important that the institution have an online library catalog you can access over the Internet so that you can easily determine what is available from the institution.

Before enrolling, ask providers the following questions so you can decide whether the library services provided will meet your needs (you will read more in Chapter 4 concerning library issues and support for the distance learner):

31 *Does the library have a toll-free telephone number?*

32 *Is there a designated librarian for distance students to contact?*

33 *Is there a "Guide to Library Resources for Distance Students"?*

34 *Is the library catalog online?*

35 *Will the library ship books and other materials to distance students?*

36 *Will the library secure books and other materials from other libraries through interlibrary loan or other means?*

37 *If so, does the library pay the fees associated with these services?*

38 *If not, what costs will you incur for having materials sent to you?*

Computer access. A computer with Internet access is rapidly becoming the essential tool for distance learners. You will have a chance to examine this topic in more detail in Chapter 3. Increasingly, distance learning programs require that students have access to a computer in order to connect to the campus by email, to receive and transmit assignments electronically, to access the online library catalog, and for many other purposes. Knowing the institution's expectations regarding computer access is an important issue for distance learners in selecting a provider.

39 *Do I need regular access to a computer?*

40 *Does the institution have clear standards on what computer capabilities I need for my degree program?*

41 *Will I need access to the Internet?*

42 *If so, does the institution provide Internet access for distance learners?*

43 *Is there a special fee for Internet access?*

The bookstore. You will need textbooks and other materials as you progress through your program. It is certainly most convenient and efficient if the institution provides bookstore services for distance students. If the institution does not provide this service, you should ask about arrangements you will need to make to secure your course materials.

44 *Does the institution have bookstore services for distance students?*

45 *If so, does the bookstore have a toll-free telephone number?*

46 *Can books be ordered online over the Internet through a secure server?*

47 *If not, how do distance students acquire course materials?*

Financial Issues

Tuition. The major expense for any program, in most cases, is the tuition. If you are attending a program in your own state, you probably qualify for in-state tuition. If you are attending a public institution out of state, you need to determine whether you are eligible for in-state tuition. Some states have set a single distance learning rate for all students, regardless of where they live. It is worth exploring this issue with each institution because the in-state tuition rate is often one-third of the out-of-state rate.

48 *If you enroll in the state in which you live, what is the tuition rate?*

49 *If you enroll as an out-of-state student, what is the tuition rate?*

Fees.   For many institutions, in recent years, fees separate from tuition have become an important source of revenue. Often special fees are assessed for technology (usually referring to computer connections), distance learning support (which pays for shipping materials to students), student activities (in which distance learning students rarely have an opportunity to participate), and library fees for distance learners. When totaled, these fees can be a substantial amount, and they should be factored in when determining the costs of a distance learning experience.

In addition to the fees charged by the institution, you may have a monthly connection fee to an Internet provider.

50 *Does the institution have fees in addition to tuition?*

51 *What are the amounts of each fee charged to distance learning students?*

Financial aid.   If you are going to require some level of financial assistance in the form of grants, scholarships, work study, or loans, be sure that the institution makes these forms of assistance available to distance students. In addition, you need to learn if the institution "counts" a distance learning student as equal to an on-campus student for financial aid purposes. Some institutions have chosen to consider distance students as only a percentage of a student taking the same load on campus. Their argument is that distance students are living at home, so they don't have commuting costs and thus their financial need is less.

52 *Does the institution award full financial aid to distance learners?*

53 *If not, for what types and level of aid are distance learners eligible?*

Student Services Issues

Admission to a program.   If your goal is a certificate or a degree, at some point you will need to seek admission to the program. Many students apply for admission to a program after they have completed several courses in order to validate their original interest in that field of study and their degree of comfort with learning at a distance. Others wish to be admitted before they take any courses so they can ensure that all courses that they complete will count toward the degree. In some professional fields, students may not be allowed to take courses until they have been admitted to the program. You don't want to begin courses at one institution and then find later that they will not transfer to the institution from which you intend to graduate.

If you have completed coursework prior to admission, whether at the institution where you are applying or elsewhere, make sure it is considered in the admission process (see the previous discussion under "Transfer Credit"). Moreover, if you feel that you have acquired prior learning through some nontraditional learning experiences, you should inquire if that can be considered in the admission process or granted after admission.

54 *Does the institution give credit for prior learning?*

55 *Does the institution allow you to "test out" of a course or courses?*

56 *Can you take courses before being admitted?*

57 *Will the institution accept transfer credits in your program?*

Registration.   An increasing number of institutions are developing alternatives to face-to-face course registration, including mail-in, online, or interactive voice response (IVR) telephone registration systems. Online and IVR systems were actually designed to speed up the process for on-campus students but they also benefit the distance learner. After you have resolved other issues related to attending at a distance, make sure that you don't have to drive to campus to register for courses.

58 *Does the institution provide options for me to register at a distance?*

Career counseling.   If you are pursuing additional education with the goal of seeking a job, changing jobs, or beginning a career, you will want to find out if career counseling services are available to distance education students. Some campus-based career centers are creating websites that list their resources. Some are willing to review electronically submitted drafts of your resume and cover letter and then provide comments.

59 *Does the institution provide access to career counseling services for distance learners?*

60 *Can you receive career counseling services at a distance?*

SUMMARY: KNOW WHAT TO EXPECT

The number of issues that have been outlined in this chapter may seem a bit overwhelming. But, they are important issues and you need to secure answers. Too many students—on or off campus—begin a college experience without really knowing what to expect. If you have answers to the questions outlined in this chapter, you shouldn't encounter many surprises during your educational journey.

 www.DLGuide.info

Visit this website for additional information and activities.

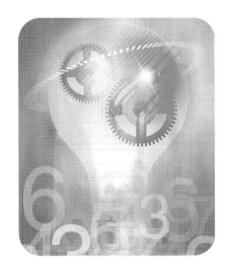

CHAPTER 3

THE ROLE OF THE COMPUTER IN DISTANCE LEARNING

Succeeding Online

In this chapter you will

- ◆ learn how computers are used in distance learning
- ◆ determine what kind of computer, accessories, and software you will need
- ◆ learn how to upgrade your existing computer or buy a suitable one
- ◆ learn how to access and use the Internet

WHY YOU NEED A COMPUTER

To participate fully in most distance learning opportunities, a computer is required. Many courses will be entirely Web delivered. You will use word-processing and other general-purpose software to prepare assignments and papers. You will also communicate with faculty members and other students; access online information resources; and perhaps use specialized computer programs for class exercises or projects, simulations, and to conduct experiments. You need to own or have regular access to a computer to complete Web-intensive courses.

Many classes that rely on videotape, CD-ROM, satellite, or printed materials may use email or the Web as the primary form of communication. For these courses, you don't have to own a computer, but you should have easy access to one.

If You Own a Computer

For those of you who own a computer, in this chapter we'll help you find out if your computer will work for online distance learning. If it won't, we'll give you some ideas to help you decide whether to upgrade your current computer or buy a new one. We'll also help you ask the right questions to get the software and hardware accessories you need for your computer.

If You Don't Own a Computer

For those of you who don't own a computer, we'll help you decide what computer to buy, and what software and hardware accessories you'll need. We'll even give you some pointers on the fine points of usage. If you can't afford a computer, we'll give you some strategies about where you might find one that you can use.

If You Are an Experienced Computer User

For those of you who are already adept at using a computer, you will find the first part of the chapter useful in understanding how computers are used for distance learning. The last part of the chapter may be useful for review.

If You Don't Feel Comfortable Using a Computer

If you've never used a computer or have used one very little, you may be concerned about using a computer to learn. Anyone contemplating taking college courses is capable of learning to use a computer. Now is the time to learn about computers—not when you are under the additional pressure of a class assignment. By taking the time to learn now, you will be more informed when the time comes to purchase a computer, and you will have more confidence when you start your program of study.

Your local library may offer basic courses on computer use. For a comprehensive introduction to computer use, consider signing up for a local adult education program at your high school or community center; these programs usually are relatively inexpensive. Community colleges and universities offer continuing education courses in a wide range of computer topics. Finally, bookstores stock numerous books on computers, and some of the larger bookstores may offer computer courses of their own.

You might want to take an informal route by working with a friend or neighbor who has a high level of computer knowledge. But recognize that your friend or neighborhood 10-year-old may know a lot about computers but be a lousy teacher. If this turns out to be the case, don't despair. Find a formal course to take and rely on your friend or neighbor to help you with problems you encounter during the learning process. Remember that the main ingredient for success is to make sure you are comfortable with basic computer use *before* you sign up for a distance learning course.

USING YOUR COMPUTER FOR DISTANCE LEARNING COURSES

The Web and Your Courses

The *Web*, also known as the *World Wide Web* or *WWW*, consists of files on millions of computers interconnected by the Internet that allow you to view text, pictures, and videos as well as hear audio.

The most popular browser is Microsoft Explorer, with Netscape as a distant second. One or both are installed on most new computers.

A website's address is called a *universal resource locator* (URL), and it usually begins http://www. or just www. Some newer sites

Self-Diagnostic Test to Determine Whether Your Computer Skills Are Up to Speed

Can you

- connect to the Internet/Web?
- use email?
- send files as an attachment?
- use a Web browser?
- bookmark a Web page?
- install new software?
- download files from the Web?
- use a word processor (such as Microsoft Word)?
- copy and paste from one document to another?

If you answer "no" to any of these questions, you need to learn the skill before taking a computer-intensive or Web course. Your distance learning provider may have its own self-diagnostic test that is specific to its courses and technology use. See the Guide's website for links to more in-depth diagnostics and online tutorials.

eliminate the www. and start with the name of the site, also called the *domain name*.

For some courses you may need to use Web browser plug-ins, which add new functions such as document delivery, audio, video, and Internet telephone. Popular plug-ins include Adobe Acrobat, Macromedia Shockwave and Flash Player, Apple Quicktime, Real Networks Real Player and Net2phone.

Your Course May Use the Web for Many Different Purposes

Course materials and information, such as a syllabus, assignments, exercises, examinations, and class discussions, may be posted on the Web. Increasingly, the Web is used as the primary way to deliver a course. If your course is delivered this way, the course website will have detailed information to supplement or replace a textbook, and extensive links to other websites to bring a wealth of information to your learning experiences. Most distance learning providers now use a course management system to organize and deliver courses. Some of the more popular course/learning management systems are Blackboard, WebCT, and eCollege.

You may take tests on the Web, either an open-book at-home test, or you may be required to come to a testing site, where a proctor can ensure the security of the testing. You may also use the Web to discuss materials by exchanging email, or by participating in a computer conference, instant messaging, or a chat room.

Courses on the Web often take full advantage of the possibilities of linking to other pages. For these courses, it is important to understand that the course is not linear like a book. It is more like searching for materials in a library, in that each new Web page leads to more pages, just as each new source in a library search can lead to another source. There is another similarity in that there are many different authors of Web pages, with different perspectives. For some students, this lack of continuity and structure makes them feel uncomfortable and ambiguous. So don't worry if you have these feelings; you're not alone. For other students, the enjoyment of surfing from one page to another is interesting and stimulating. Be careful, though, not to get lost in following links too far from the faculty member's intentions. If you do get lost, remember that you can always go back to your home page by clicking on the "Home" button at the top of the screen, or to your course page by clicking on its bookmark.

The Web contains information of all sorts, from factual to unsubstantiated to intentionally incorrect. Some information is ultra conservative and some ultraliberal. There are religious sites and pornographic sites. You need to be cautious and carefully evaluate all the information you find on the Web. For more information on researching, see Chapter 4.

Online Course Discussions

The most common discussion tool is a threaded discussion or computer conference organized so that it is easy to follow a topic of discussion from start to finish. It is similar to email, except the messages in a threaded discussion are arranged by topic whereas most email programs organize the messages by the date and time the message was sent. Each student reads and makes his or her comments over a period of time, from a day to several weeks.

Taking a Course on a Course or Learning Management System

A course or learning management system organizes, standardizes, and automates Web course delivery.

- The advantage for the learner is that the courses offered by the distance learning provider all use the same type of basic class structure, delivery of assignments and method of paper submission, threaded discussions, instant messaging, chat room, testing, and other tools.

- Classes may be accessed only by registered class members by using a logon or user name and password. This ensures that any discussions of sensitive class materials remain private.

Another common discussion method is email, usually using a Listserv. The faculty member or a student either starts a discussion by typing a message on a new topic or responds to messages that others have sent.

You may also use an instant messaging system or chat room to "talk" to other students by typing messages on your computer. The writing appears immediately on each participant's screen. In distance learning, these messaging systems are used for discussions by the whole class as well as for team or group work. Chat rooms allow smaller groups to talk to each other in a separate virtual space. Examples of instant messaging systems include AOL Instant Messenger, Microsoft Net Meeting and MSN Messenger, ICQ (shorthand for I seek you), and a variety of Web-based software included as part of the course management system your distance learning provider uses.

Email, Threaded Discussion, and Listserv Tips

All email packages, threaded discussions, and Listservs have their differences, but all use messages similar to email to communicate. There are some universal tips for using them:

- Try to look at each message just once. Read it, and reply if needed. You may keep it, print it, or delete it.
- If you find it tiresome to read long documents on a computer screen, consider printing lengthy course information documents.

Power-User Tips on Using the Web

- To conduct a search for information, click on the "Search" button and follow the on-screen instructions. There are many search sites on the Web, and your browser will have a default already selected. To find other Web search sites, do a search using "search engines" as the search words. You can also search by name for some current favorites: Google, Yahoo!, Microsoft Network (MSN), America Online (AOL), and Ask Jeeves.
- If you get a Web address (URL) in an email, highlight the address, copy it, and then switch to your browser and "paste" it into the browser's address area. This way you avoid making errors in writing it down and retyping it.
- Click the "Back" button at the top of the screen to back up one page at a time. But to go back two, three, or more Web pages, use the history function to look at all the recent pages and choose one.
- Bookmark the pages you think you will use frequently. While the Web page you want to bookmark is on your computer screen, click "Favorites" then "Add Favorite" in Internet Explorer or the equivalent command from the menu. Or, you can left click on the icon to the left of the address, drag it over to the "Favorites" button, and when it opens the "Favorites" menu, drop the item in the location you want. Another option is to right click on a link on the page and then choose from the pop-up menu "Add Favorite."
- If you want to follow a link but keep the original page easily accessible, right click on a link in the Web page. A menu will pop up and you will be given the choice of opening that link in a new window.
- For other power-user tips, go to the Guide's website for links to tutorials offered by Internet Explorer and Netscape.

For information that you want to keep handy to review or study in depth, a loose-leaf binder or folder works well for organizing printed pages.

- If you have multiple classes using email or belong to multiple Listservs, automatically send each email to a different folder on your computer, if your mail program supports it. This is usually called filtering. Each email program does this a little differently, so be sure to read your email manual or use the help function in your email. Filtering makes it easier to work with each course and ensures continuity within a folder. (This tip does not apply to threaded discussions.)

- When you originate or reply to a message, try to keep it short, ideally one computer screen in length, unless your instructor has specified a length. Long messages are difficult to read on a computer screen and remember.

- If you have a number of points to make on different subjects, send them out in separate messages over a few hours, days, or a week. This also increases the number of posts, which is helpful if your instructor is keeping track.

- When replying to messages, keep only the passage or paragraph of the original email that is relative to your response. Keeping emails concise and to the point saves time for other students and the instructor and keeps them from becoming frustrated over sorting through unnecessary text.

- Make sure you participate regularly. Your course instructor may keep all your email messages and use them for your grade, looking at the quality of your postings, and even the number of postings over the length of the course.

- Remember that in email and web courses, everyone can participate in discussions. In a traditional course, those who think fast or like to talk often dominate discussion. In electronic discussions, you can take the time to think about the points you want to make or questions to ask and phrase them exactly the way you want. You can jump in early or wait until the end to try to have the last word.

- If you want to make sure your emails containing comments, questions, assignments, or papers are received by your instructor or a listserv, use one of the newer email programs that allow you to request delivery confirmation. You can request that a confirmation be sent when your instructor's or the Listserv's computer receives the email. A confirmation can also be sent when the instructor reads the email. Before you rely on this method, though, make sure your instructor's email program provides confirmations. Remember that Listservs do not return confirmations from individual subscribers. Another simpler way to check whether your email was sent is to send a copy to yourself by adding your email address in the Cc: or Bcc: address lines. Although this will not ensure that your instructor has received or read your email, it can alleviate concerns that your email program or Internet connection may not be functioning correctly.

- Remember that although email is informal, and occasional misspellings and lapses in grammar are tolerated on the Internet, in a class you will probably be held to a higher standard. For classes, use standard business letter formatting, including skipping a line between paragraphs, and use proper grammar, punctuation, and sentence structure.

Listservs

Listservs use the Internet to distribute email to groups of people, sometimes even thousands of individuals. Some courses use Listservs to distribute emails from one student, or the instructor, to all the other members of the class. "Discussions" by all the class members, and "question-and-answer sessions" between the instructor or a guest "speaker" and the students are facilitated using Listservs. Most institutions will sign you up for the class Listserv. If an institution expects you to subscribe yourself, it will provide directions. Once subscribed, you may send an email to the list address and the Listserv computer will send it out to all subscribers automatically.

Usually, Listservs have an address where you can send commands such as "subscribe" and "unsubscribe." Many people make the mistake of trying to send these commands to the same address where they send regular email. In doing so, everyone on the Listserv gets the subscribe and unsubscribe commands intended for the command address, which can be annoying because members then have to open or delete the message. Don't make this mistake! And when someone else makes this mistake, don't send an email about it—it only generates more junk email.

Netiquette

Netiquette is a contraction of Inter*net* and *etiquette*. It is the code of conduct for getting along with other Inter*net* citizens, or *netizens*. Here are some of the rules to be observed:

- Do not use profanity or make negative or hurtful comments about other students' comments or work. This is called *flaming*. If you are angry or frustrated when you write your email, save it

Email and Internet Addresses Explained

An email address consists of a minimum of five parts:

1. the person's logon, or user name
2. the symbol @
3. the organization's name, also known as the second-level domain name
4. a period separating each domain name
5. the type of organization, or top-level domain name

For example, student Amy Smith taking courses from Ivy League University in the United States might have this address:

asmith@ivyu.edu

in which "asmith" is Amy Smith's logon or user name, "@" separates the user name from the domain names, ivyu is the second-level domain name of Ivy League University, and edu is the top-level domain name.

There can be third-level domain names, too, such as

asmith@college.ivyu.edu

in which college is the third-level domain name.

Web addresses take a similar form with a minimum of three parts:

1. WWW (optional) followed by a period
2. the organization's second-level domain name followed by a period
3. the type of organization, or top-level domain name

Ivy League University might have the following main Web page name:

www.ivyu.edu

Note that the http:// often found in front of the Web address is not part of the address, and with most Web browsers it is not necessary for you to type it.

> There are many top-level domain names, with new ones frequently added. Some examples of these domain names and their affiliations are as follows:
>
> - edu—<u>edu</u>cational, colleges and universities
> - com—<u>com</u>mercial, for-profit businesses
> - org—<u>org</u>anization, a nonprofit organization
> - info—<u>info</u>rmation, for organizations
> - gov—<u>gov</u>ernment, United States
> - biz—<u>com</u>mercial, for-profit businesses
> - mil—<u>mil</u>itary, United States
> - us—any organization based in the United States
> - fr—<u>Fr</u>ance

until the next day if possible, and then eliminate the negative language and be sure the tone is appropriate.

- Do not write in all caps unless you need to emphasize a point, and never use all caps when writing to your instructors. In Internet culture, writing in all caps tells others that you are angry.

- Do not expect an instantaneous answer to your email or other posting. Many instructors will indicate how frequently they check their email. Some class members may answer very quickly, whereas others may take days or even a week. Just because your email was sent almost instantaneously doesn't mean that the person it was sent to was available and ready to answer the moment it was received.

- Think carefully about the relevance of information to the recipient. The auto-addressing functions provided in email programs make it easy to send the same email to many people. It can sometimes be tempting to do this "just in case they are interested." This is fine if it's your friends or mother, but not necessarily for your fellow students or faculty. They might view information that has nothing to do with the class purpose as a waste of time.

There are many other Internet culture issues. To learn about them, conduct a Web search of the word "netiquette."

Internet Discussion Groups

The easiest way to gain new information and to understand the culture of a field or specialty within a field is to subscribe to a discussion group to read the postings. Some Listservs do not require you to sign up to post to the group, but most are moderated and screen postings to ensure that they are on topic, to prevent "spam" or block objectionable material. Before you post to a Listserv, it's a good idea to spend some time just reading messages, known as *lurking,* until you understand the culture and scope of the group. It is a breach of netiquette to post messages that are not appropriate to a group's topic, and appropriateness varies by the Listserv. Often prior discussions from the Listserv are archived on a website so that members (and often nonmembers) may research a topic to see if that topic has been discussed in the past. It is considered bad form to sign up for a Listserv and immediately ask the standard "newbie" questions, so either lurk or read the archives.

In your course work, you may want to post a question to a discussion group to get some expert information. There are experts out there who may provide excellent information, but beware that there are also those who possess less subject knowledge than you yet are more than happy to play the expert.

Video and Audio on Your Computer

Almost all computer packages have a standard computer display, which includes speakers for audio and video playback capability. Currently, phone lines have the capacity to carry acceptable quality audio along with the other computer signals on a modem connection. For instructional purposes, the video currently available over telephone lines is suitable for some limited purposes. High-bandwidth (fast) Internet connections such as digital subscriber line (DSL), cable TV, and satellite are capable of quality real-time video, but Internet congestion at any point in the connection path can disrupt the video for a period of time, resulting in a "buffering" pause. For those without a high-bandwidth connection, reasonable quality motion video is limited.

Audio includes playing back prerecorded sound, live streamed sound, and telephone on your computer. Examples of educational prerecorded or live streamed sound audio include lectures by faculty members; talks given by guest speakers; and sounds that illustrate important points in instruction such as musical phrases for a music appreciation course, speech impediments for a speech therapy class, or announcer styles for a TV production class. In some courses, you may be asked to record a speech for a foreign language course or a television production class, or to annotate a text report for clarity. Internet or IP "telephone" allows multiple students to have simultaneous course discussions among themselves or work on group projects. The instructor can lead a discussion or review session.

Video capability can provide recorded video programs that supplement the course materials, provide lectures by well-known authorities, or add film or TV clips. Recorded video can be played from a CD-ROM in your computer, or over the Internet if your connection is "fast." If the students and instructor have cameras on their computers, called desktop videoconferencing, they can all see each other while they discuss course issues. Video over the Internet remains cumbersome, but new methods and faster connections will continue to make it more commonplace.

Submitting Your Assignments by Computer

Some distance learning providers have students mail assignments to them. Using a computer provides several faster ways for you to submit your work and then receive it after your instructor has graded it. You can send email, using plain text and attachments; fax; post to the Web; and use File Transfer Protocol (FTP). Your instructor will tell you which methods you may use in each course. It's a good idea to send a test message far in advance of the due date of the assignment if it's the first time that you've attempted these methods of submission.

The basic way to email your work to your instructor is to write the assignment or paper as a regular email. However, some email programs do not have good word-processing capabilities, so you may wish to write in your word processor and copy the text over to an email screen. To do this, while in your word  processor, highlight all the text you want to send and use the copy command to copy it to your computer's memory. Then go to your email program and address a new email message to your instructor.

Next use the paste function to place the copied text in the message. Be sure to check that it all copied and then send it. Word-processed documents may lose their formatting, such as tabs, bold, and underlining, when you use this method. Spreadsheets and databases cannot be sent this way.

Email attachments, sometimes called enclosures, are becoming the preferred way to send text and can be used to send spreadsheets and databases. To use email attachments, both your email program and the instructor's must be capable of handling attachments, and the instructor must have the same software (e. g., word processor) you used to create the document. First you must complete your work in the word processor, spreadsheet, database, or specialized program and save the file. Be sure to remember or write down the file name. Then go to your email program and start composing a new email to your instructor. Explain what the email attachment is in the body of the email. Then attach the document you saved using whatever method your email requires.

You may use your modem to fax documents directly from the computer without printing them out. When your document is ready to send, change the printer selection in the print menu to your fax modem. When you print, it prints to the modem and the modem will walk you through how to fax it. Make sure you have your instructor's fax number handy when you start this process.

An older method of exchanging files is FTP. Some distance learning programs use FTP for student assignments and papers. When using FTP, complete your work and save the file. Remember or write down the file name. Then start the FTP program and follow the instructions to send the file. Your instructor will give you an address to a directory, or perhaps to a Web page, where you will send your work. If you don't have an FTP program, you may download one from the Internet. Using FTP may require some help from your distance learning provider's help desk or your instructor.

Other Technologies You May Use

Distance learning providers frequently mix technologies in the same course and degree program. For example, even if your course is primarily computer based, you may need to use a VCR to watch videotapes and either a speakerphone or an IP telephone headset for long audio-conferences with other students and the instructor. In some cases, you may need to travel to a location to view a satellite broadcast or to participate in a videoconference. Increasingly, all of these experiences—audioconferences with others and full-motion, high-quality video both recorded and live—will be possible using just your computer.

WHAT KIND OF COMPUTER IS REQUIRED FOR COLLEGE COURSES?

What kind of computer will you need? Usually, a computer that can connect to the Internet and use the most recent browsers is a minimum. More information about computer requirements is usually available in the printed institutional marketing materials. Or if a computer is available to you, connect to the Internet and look at the distance learning institution's Web page for computer information. If it doesn't list the computer requirements, it should have an email address where you can ask questions. You may prefer to call and ask the institution you're considering what the minimum and preferred computer specifications are for the class or the degree program in which you are interested. A toll-free phone number indicates that an institution may be "student friendly." However, if the institution can't answer your questions, this could be an indication that it might not be student friendly. How the institution responds to your questions may help you to decide whether to enroll in its courses.

Keep in mind that if you are working on a degree with one institution, you may eventually complete it with another. It is therefore a good idea to check the computer requirements of more than one college or university. Also keep in mind that technology changes quickly, so requirements may change from semester to semester.

Another way to decide what kind of computer you'll need is to find out what software you will use in your courses and use that information to evaluate your options. Most software packaging states the minimum computer capabilities for running the software. You'll want to buy or upgrade to a higher level than the minimum. This will ensure that the software runs quickly and smoothly from the beginning and will allow new versions of the same software to run smoothly. New versions usually require more computing power to run at the same speed.

Questions to Ask Distance Education Providers

(Visit the Guide's website for a succinct checklist of questions.)

Operating system. Every computer has an operating system that allows all the applications software, such as word processors and spreadsheets, to work. Most personal computers (PCs) use a version of Microsoft Windows or Apple Macintosh OS (Mac OS). When you decide to buy a computer, which operating system to buy is already decided for you. If you buy a windows PC, you will be using a version of Microsoft Windows, and if you buy a Macintosh, you will be using a version of Mac OS. Note that there are many more windows computers than there are Macintosh computers.

1 *What version of Microsoft Windows or Apple Macintosh operating system do you recommend?*

Processor. The processor, also known as the microprocessor or central processing unit (CPU), is the "brain" of the computer. A fast processor allows programs or files to load in your computer faster, saving you "wait time." New versions of software usually require a faster processor to load and operate at the same speed as the old version. The higher the number of a processor, the faster it is. Processor speed is usually stated as gigahertz (GHz), such as 2.3 GHz.

2 *What is the minimum and preferred processor type and speed?*

RAM. The memory in a computer is called random access memory (RAM). This memory is where the operating system, software, and the data you type in are stored while you are working. More RAM allows your computer to work faster, thus reducing your waiting time. RAM size is stated as megabytes (MB), such as 512 MB.

3 *What is the minimum memory capacity, or RAM?*

Hard disk space. When you turn off your computer, the information, such as the operating system, software programs, and your data files (e.g., papers and assignments), is stored on the hard disk for later use. Hard disk capacity is usually stated in gigabytes (GB). When you ask your distance learning provider how much disk space is needed for your class, you're not asking what the overall size of disk drive you'll need should be. You are asking how much more space the required programs need (if you don't already have them on your computer), plus the space needed for data files.

4 *How much, if any, hard disk space is required?*

CD-ROM. Some distance learning programs use a CD-ROM for course materials.

5 *Is a CD-ROM needed?*

Modem speed.   A modem and telephone line are used to connect to the Internet. The faster the modem the less time you'll wait for information to transfer between your computer and another. High-speed connections such as DSL, cable TV, or satellite may be required by some distance learning providers or programs.

6 *What is the minimum and preferred modem speed?*

Multimedia.   Audio and video accessories, peripherals, or software may be needed for some programs.

7 *Do the courses require any special multimedia equipment or software?*

Microphone/video camera.   Some courses may require you to participate in discussions over the Internet. These discussions may be just voice, similar to the telephone, or include video so that you can both see and hear the other members of your class.

8 *Do I need a sound card, microphone, telephone headset, or desktop video camera?*

Internet access.   To access the Web or exchange email you will need Internet access via a modem, DSL, cable TV, or satellite.

9 *Does the institution provide access to the Internet through local or toll-free numbers?*

10 *If not, does the institution have discounts with any Internet service providers (ISPs)?*

Computer access.   If you know you will need to purchase a computer, the easiest way to buy it may be through a special program. You get exactly what you need with a minimum of stress.

11 *Does the institution have any special programs through which I can purchase or lease a computer?*

Software requirements.   Software, or computer programs, have specific functions, such as typing papers and assignments (word processor), accessing multimedia on the Internet (Web browser), or mathematical or financial calculations (spreadsheets).

12 *What software does the institution require?*

Some distance learning providers require specialized software. You will need to know where and how to get this software. Some providers may send it to you on a disk or CD. or you may have to buy it from a bookstore or download it from the Internet.

13 *Is there specialized course software?*

14 *If yes, how do I get it? Is it available for the Macintosh computer (if applicable)?*

Assignment submission. Most courses require the submission of assignments or papers. There are a number of options for submitting assignments: printing out and mailing, faxing, sending email attachments/enclosures using FTP, or posting to the course website.

15 *How will I turn in assignments?*

Computer longevity. Since most degrees take at least two years to complete, and perhaps more if you're going to school part-time, it is helpful to know how long the computer that meets today's needs will last.

16 *How many years will the minimum and preferred computer configurations the institution recommends be capable of being used for its courses?*

If the acceptable use period of the computer is less than the time it will take you to complete the courses or degree you desire, factor part of the cost of a computer upgrade or replacement into the cost of the instruction. Also, remember that you use or will use your computer for other lifestyle purposes, so don't think of the total cost as entirely for your studies.

In general, you will use the previous information and the checklist to evaluate your current computer or purchase a new computer. Specifically, minimum recommendations should be considered when evaluating your current computer to determine whether it is suitable, needs to be upgraded, or needs to be replaced. Preferred recommendations should be considered when buying a new computer (see the section "Checklist for Purchasing a New Computer").

Deciding Whether to Upgrade or Buy a New Computer

In general, you shouldn't upgrade a computer because computer technology advances so fast that inexpensive upgrades never bring your computer up to current standards. But this is not necessarily the case for distance learning purposes. If you need to add some new equipment (e.g., a telephone headset) or software, and your computer can accommodate the requirements, upgrading may be worthwhile. However, if your computer is more than a few years old, the processor is too slow, or the hard drive has too little storage space, it probably would be better to buy a new computer.

If your computer monitor (screen) still works well and has a good picture, you may be able to use it with a new computer. If you want to give the old computer to a child, parent, or friend, you may want to buy a new monitor along with the new computer. Many mass-market stores bundle complete computer systems with a monitor and printer. Most computer stores and online companies sell complete systems and systems with minimal accessories such as a keyboard, mouse, and speakers.

What's in Your Current Computer?

Once you know what minimum and preferred hardware your distance learning provider recommends, find out what's inside your current computer: the type of processor, the amount of RAM, and the hardware components. The easiest way is to look at the original receipt. If it doesn't provide the necessary information, go to the control panel of your computer and look in the system properties files. Or, simpler still, call the help desk or technical support at the distance learning provider and ask for assistance in determining the hardware configuration you currently have.

SHOPPING FOR COMPUTING EQUIPMENT AND SOFTWARE

Do your homework before shopping. Read computer and consumer magazines for reviews of computer equipment and software. Only read reviews for the last three months because computers change so fast. Before shopping for a computer, answer the following questions using the information you receive from your distance learning institution.

Checklist for Purchasing a New Computer

(Visit the Guide's website for these questions.)

WHAT HARDWARE WILL YOU NEED?

- **Windows or Macintosh Operating System?** If your distance learning provider does not indicate a preference of operating system, a Windows system may make the most sense. Currently, Windows computers account for more than 95 percent of sales, whereas Macintosh computers account for less than 5 percent.

Fewer stores understand and can support Macintosh computers. These computers are prevalent in the arts and education career fields. The Windows operating system is dominant in other areas. Most popular programs are available for both systems.

- **Desktop or Notebook?** First, think about whether you want a desktop computer or a notebook computer, sometimes called a laptop. A desktop computer is less expensive and the screen is larger and easier to read. The full-size mouse is easier to use and the keyboard is more comfortable for long-term use. However, a desktop computer means sitting at a desk. By contrast, a notebook allows you to work anytime, anyplace without being tied to a desk. If you travel frequently, or will study most of the time away from home, a notebook may be best for you. Keep in mind, though, that to access the Web or your email, a phone line, wireless network, or high-speed Internet connection must be available at locations away from home. Most hotel rooms have a data port on the room phone or you can disconnect the telephone and plug in your modem cord. Airports have phones with data jacks that work with a modem, but most other locations may prove difficult. Many businesses have digital phone lines that modems cannot use, but they may have spare network connections that you can plug into if your notebook computer has an Ethernet port. In addition, many hotels and airports have wireless networks that can provide convenient online access points if you have a wireless PC card in your notebook computer. Acessories for notebooks are more expensive and more prone to damage and theft. Batteries are expensive, don't last very long, and plugging into the wall for power defeats some of the purposes of having a notebook. For a few hundred dollars extra you can buy a desktop monitor, full-size keyboard, and mouse for your notebook and have both capabilities.

- **Screen Size?** If you opt for a desktop computer, the size of the monitor you buy is important. A 15-inch monitor is acceptable but a 17-inch monitor is better. Larger screen size on a notebook is desirable but often costs considerably more and makes the notebook heavier and bulkier.

- **Buy from the Campus?** Some distance learning institutions sell computers; others have relationships with mail-order brand-name companies such as Dell and Gateway. Buying a computer this way is easy because the exact computer needed for your courses is specified, and you'll get a reasonable price.

- **Brand Name or Generic?** Brand-name computers are slightly more expensive than generic or clone computers. Computers are all made of the same components: case; power supply; motherboard (the heart of the computer), usually with modem and Ethernet connections built in; hard-disk drive (storage inside the computer for programs and files); 3.5-inch floppy disk drive (which uses computer disks that allow you to transport files from your computer to another); and CD-ROM. Factories build most brand-name computers, whereas local stores and mail-order companies build most generic computers. If quality components are used, any computer should work well and last for its technological lifetime of two to five years. Technical support for brand-name computers is always available. However, technical support for generic computers depends on the stability of the company from which you buy it. Many are "here today, gone tomorrow." If you have little knowledge about computers, or are not prepared to learn about them, purchasing a generic computer is risky.

- **Buy Used?** Used computers are frequently available, but for the most part should be avoided. Computers for sale are often found in classified ads, but the prices are almost always too high, because these computers are usually obsolete or very nearly so. There is also the risk of purchasing a stolen computer through these ads. It's best not to buy a computer from someone you don't know. Stores may occasionally sell used or refurbished computers, but buying these can also be risky because they may be "lemons" returned by other customers.

- **Buy from a Discount Store?** Local discount stores provide brand-name computers at reasonable cost. However, the employees often are not knowledgeable, and after-sales support is usually not available or minimal.

- **Buy from a Mail-Order Company?** Large customer-focused mail-order companies such as Dell generally have good customer support before and after the sale, but you will pay a little more than from a smaller company that just sells computers in a box without the additional services. The cheapest price for a name-brand computer will be from a mail-order "box-only" company. But don't expect much help on the telephone. Generally, you must know exactly what you need to be successful in purchasing from such companies. After-sale support generally is not available.

- **Computer Monitor Included?** A computer monitor is often included in the price of the computer. However, you can buy your computer from one dealer and the monitor from another without concern about compatibility. Some stores sell packages, or "bundles," that include the monitor and a printer, and these package deals may be worthwhile. Sometimes stores will advertise a low price on a computer knowing that they can make their profit on the monitor. Price shop and carefully evaluate both the package and individual prices.

- **Scanner?** Unless you buy a scanner, you will not be able to fax originals, such as hand-written notes and drawings, that are not a file on your computer. There are two other options for faxing: you may choose to buy a fax machine or use a local copy center to fax at a per-page rate. If your instructor will be faxing your graded work to you, you should either leave your computer on all the time in auto fax receive mode or arrange to be called before a fax is sent. Both options are cumbersome, so you may wish to consider having your work faxed back to a local copy center or other business.

- **Buying a Printer?** If you need a printer, look for a bundle that includes it. Keep in mind that the least expensive printer is not always the one with the lowest price tag. The total cost of ownership needs to be considered. The operating cost per page for an inkjet (black and color) printer is usually more than for a laser (black) printer. Although the most inexpensive printers will suit your needs for your classes, you need to consider other uses as well. Do you require sharper images and faster printing times? If so, you may find that a more expensive printer is the better choice.

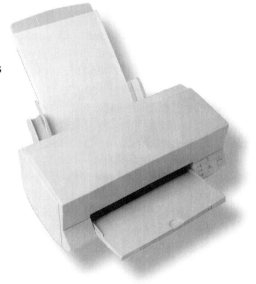

- **Accessories?** Some distance learning programs may require additional peripherals such as a microphone to record your voice, or a telephone headset to discuss issues over the Internet (like a phone call). Increasingly, courses use cameras that are placed on top of the computer monitor so you can video teleconference with the other students and faculty in your class.

- **Paper or Plastic?** Always pay by credit card for computer purchases (or for any costly items) because the credit card provider gives extra protection and help if something goes wrong with the transaction or the computer.

WHAT SOFTWARE WILL YOU NEED?

At a minimum, you'll probably need the following essential software:

- ☑ a word processor to write papers, reports, letters, and other documents
- ☑ a Web browser to access websites on the Internet
- ☑ an email package if you're not going to use the email functions in the Web browser

You also may need:

- ☑ a presentation program (such as Microsoft PowerPoint) for organizing and presenting class projects and reports
- ☑ a spreadsheet program (such as Microsoft Excel) to work with numbers and budgets
- ☑ a database program to organize data for projects or research
- ☑ plug-ins, or small programs, to bring new capabilities to your Web browser
- ☑ specialized software required by the distance learning institution

Software suites, such as Microsoft Office, combine programs for word processing, spreadsheets, databases, and presentations into a single package and are normally already installed on a computer when you buy it.

Can't Afford a Computer?

If you can't afford to buy a computer at this time but want to take a class, check into using a friend's computer or the library's public access computers. If your employer has Internet access, ask to use a computer after regular work hours. If you are planning to be a full-time student, the distance learning institution may be able to provide a scholarship, loan, or other financial aid to help you buy a computer.

Many campus credit unions have special low rates for computer purchases. Many mail-order companies now provide lease/purchase options with monthly payments. At the end of the lease, you either pay a small amount to keep the computer or get a new computer and continue your payments.

SELECTING AN INTERNET SERVICE PROVIDER (ISP)

Checklist for selecting an ISP

☑ Some distance learning institutions have toll-free numbers to a modem pool that you can access at no cost. If so, you can dial in to connect with the campus and the Internet/Web.

☑ If you don't live close to the campus, you'll need a company—an ISP—that connects you to the Internet and the Web through either a modem, DSL (a kind of high-speed phone line), cable TV, or satellite. If your distance learning institution doesn't have a discount arranged with an ISP, ask friends what ISP they use or check your local Yellow Pages under "Internet" or "computers" for ISPs.

☑ Choose an ISP that provides the highest speed you can afford if you will be taking Web-based courses. You will spend less time waiting for course modules to download, or when doing research on the Web. Cable TV companies, DSL, and satellite provide Internet access at a much higher speed than regular telephone ISPs. If high-speed service is available in your area, and you can afford the extra expense, you should take advantage of it.

☑ Telephone dial-up ISPs charge for connect time in two ways. The most common is unlimited connect time for a monthly flat fee. The other is a flat charge for a number of hours, with extra hours at additional cost. The institution through which you're taking courses should be able to tell you about how many hours per week you will need for a given course. Remember, too, that you probably will use the Web for more than course work, and plan accordingly.

☑ Avoid modem ISPs that cut costs by keeping the number of phone lines for you to dial into too low. This results in frequent busy signals, especially during the more popular evening and weekend times.

☑ DSL, cable TV, and satellite connections are full-time, and always connected, so they charge a flat fee per month.

☑ If you own a notebook and travel overnight frequently, you may want to pick a national or international ISP so that you can dial in without long distance charges from your hotel.

☑ There are national providers, such as America On-Line (AOL), Earthlink, and Microsoft Network (MSN), that provide access to the Internet along with their own services, such as websites with entertaining information and chat rooms. The additional services are usually more expensive and are not necessary for your distance learning courses.

☑ A good ISP should have readily accessible technical support at the times you will be working. Technical support available 24 hours a day, 7 days a week (24 by 7) is best, especially if your connection dies in the middle of writing that last-minute paper.

☑ Most ISPs provide an email account as part of the service. If you have additional family members, ask the ISP if it will provide free email accounts for them as well.

☑ If you have a Macintosh computer, make sure the ISP's technical support staff is familiar with them since they are not as common as Windows computers.

☑ When you sign up for an ISP, you will be given a user name and password. You should also be provided with instructions on how to connect to the ISP and get your email. Some ISPs will provide a Web home page where you can display information about yourself, your interests, or your expertise. When you register for a distance learning class, the institution may also give you a user name and password and require you to use it. If so, you can use the email address provided by the institution with any ISP connection.

ARE YOU READY FOR ONLINE COURSES?

The final test to see if you're ready for your online class: connect to the Guide's Distance Learner website. You'll find updated information, especially on continually changing parts of the book, such as this chapter. Happy Web surfing!

Amy Goes to Ivy League University . . . and Stays at Home

Amy is a single mother of two who wants to improve her job skills. She decides that she is going to seek a degree at Ivy League University. She chooses Ivy League over several others because of its reputation and affordable cost after financial aid, and because it seems to be student friendly. She won't have to go to a campus every week, and with two children, that's important.

Ivy League recommends that she buy a copy of *The Distance Learner's Guide*. After reading it, Amy goes to her local library to use the Web. With the help of her 12-year-old daughter, Maggie, she goes to the Guide's website and looks at up-to-the-minute information about resources available to her.

Since she hasn't used a computer much and doesn't own one, Amy prints out a copy of the computer-related checklists on the website: "Questions to Ask Distance Education Providers," "Purchasing a New Computer," and "Selecting an Internet Service Provider (ISP)." First she phones Ivy League and asks the questions on the "Questions to Ask Distance Education Providers" checklist. She finds out that she needs a Windows computer capable of running the latest version of the Internet Explorer Web browser. Since she plans to get a new computer, she knows she'll have plenty of hard disk space. The computer she plans to buy will also need a CD-ROM drive, a modem, Microsoft Office XP software suite (Word word processor, Excel spreadsheet, Access database, and Powerpoint presentation software), Eudora email, Adobe Acrobat document software, and a Real Audio browser plug-in. Ivy League will send a CD-ROM disk with video segments for one of her classes. Ivy League arranges for discounted ISP access but recommends that Amy shop around to see if she can find a less expensive option. She will turn in her assignments and papers in the way specified by each of her instructors, either faxing them directly from her computer or sending them as email attachments. Ivy League is not willing to commit to how long the computer will be suitable for her but speculates "at least two years." Ivy League informs Amy that she can buy exactly the computer she wants from its on-campus computer store.

Since her finances are tight, Amy uses the information she receives from Ivy League, along with information from reading this chapter, to call the campus computer store as well as a large national mail-order company and to visit a local mass-market department store. She fills out a separate checklist for each. Amy decides to buy from the campus store because the cost is about the same, and she feels it will provide the best service. She purchases the minimum recommended computer along with a printer so she can print out long course messages and her children can use it to print out school projects.

While Amy awaits the arrival of her computer, she talks with her good friends, Marcia and Beth, who have computers with Internet access. Both friends agree that there are several good local ISPs, but they are both paying more than Ivy League's discounted national Internet provider charges. Amy calls the national provider and arranges for service. The provider tells her that a CD will be sent so she can set up her computer for service.

The computer arrives a few days later and Amy asks Russ, a friend, to help her set it up. She is surprised how easily everything connects—the cables only fit one way. Her 16-year-old son, Matt, helps.

Amy is not so lucky with the Internet access. She sets up her computer software with the CD the ISP sends her, but it doesn't work. Although it is 10 P.M.—she didn't have time until the children were asleep—someone at the ISP's technical support number answers after a 15-minute wait and walks her through the setup. Since Amy doesn't have a second telephone line for her computer, she has to hang up to test the setup. She follows the process for connecting, and it works!

The first place Amy goes is the website for her first course. There is a message from the instructor welcoming the class and telling everyone to check their email. Amy finds she has email from two of her instructors again welcoming her and also asking that she respond with a short paragraph about herself.

The next day, Amy tells her friend Marcia, "I wasn't sure I could do this, but now I know I can. I've been out of school for a long time. Even the computer seemed scary at first, but it's much easier than I thought."

SUMMARY: QUESTIONS TO ASK PROSPECTIVE DISTANCE EDUCATION PROVIDERS

1. How many hours per week will I need to use a computer?
2. How many hours per week will I need to be connected to the Internet?
3. What kind of computer will I need?

4. How many years will I be able to use the computer you recommend for your distance learning courses?
5. What peripherals and accessories do I need?
6. What software will I need?
7. Do you have recommendations about where to buy my computer, accessories, or software?
8. Do you provide Internet access or have a discount plan with an ISP?
9. Is financial aid available to help pay for computer-related costs?
10. What kind of technical support do you provide? Telephone, fax, email, or Web support? What hours is support available?

---

www.DLGuide.info

Visit this website for additional information and activities.

CHAPTER 4

THE DISTANCE LEARNER'S LIBRARY

The Indispensable Guide to Finding Quality Resources

In this chapter you will

- ◆ learn how to locate library resources available at your institution—even if you never set foot on campus
- ◆ discover how to find resources in other libraries
- ◆ find out how to navigate your way around the Internet for quality information

In the sixteenth century, the first scholarly libraries of England, Cambridge and Oxford, were replete with manuscripts, scrolls, tablets, and books containing the world's knowledge and ideas. When scholars needed access to the recorded information and ideas of the day, they had to spend a lot of time in the library's reading room. There was no other choice, because in those days it was common to physically chain the books to the shelves! Scholars literally burned the late-night candles to further their learning. The idea of a public lending library didn't appear until the eighteenth century.

The library reading rooms of today are still busy places, and, fortunately, the books are no longer chained to the shelves. The ancient library stood alone, collecting—and carefully protecting—the books and documents in its possession. The modern library is part of an international network, collecting and exchanging material with others, and offering a rich array of information online.

The print and media materials in our current libraries are now searchable from computerized catalogs. These online catalogs may be a mix of resources owned by the library and may contain items in nearby libraries that are part of the same library consortium or regional system. Some of the records in the online catalog may have imbedded Web links that point to freely accessible Web resources or to leased resources purchased by the library and controlled through license agreements. Other databases available at library websites instantly link you to many journals, newspaper files, and government publications online. These database services may offer you the option of downloading or emailing articles and documents to your computer, or receiving them by fax.

You will find not only that many materials are available online, but that librarians are available as well. Besides the traditional call-in phone numbers to the reference desk, many libraries allow you to post email questions any time of the day or night. Some libraries are even experimenting with new remote reference software programs that allow them to chat with you in real time and even "push" Web pages and documents right to your computer. This is more advanced than email reference, in which you have to wait an unknown period of time to receive an answer. Virtual reference is "live" reference and interactive. It's much more like a consulting session. Libraries are grouping together to share professional assistance online; librarians from each institution sign up for designated hours on the virtual reference desk to help anyone sending questions online.

Today's library is a major key to the information age, and today's librarians may be the distance learner's best friends. Most librarians have a broad knowledge of information access tools, but most also specialize in certain areas. This is particularly true in large universities, which may have different branches for science or medical collections, and sometimes separate law libraries. But even in smaller college libraries, you will find that you may be passed on to the government information specialist or science librarian if the first person you speak with doesn't have ready knowledge of your research area.

Still, not every library can be equally responsive, not every online source is equally authoritative, and some services can cost you money that you need not spend. This chapter briefs you on what modern libraries and information sources can do, and why some of them can serve you better than others. We suggest some questions for you to ask and point out some sources you can use.

The bottom line is this: as you choose a distance learning program, an obvious question is, "Can I really take the courses from here, where I am?" More often than not, an important part of that question is, "Can I really get the library services that I'll need here, where I am?" Good libraries and related information services are more available, have more material to offer, and are better prepared to work with you than ever before. So rather than having books chained to shelves, access to information is only limited by your ability to access the Internet. And wireless technologies are making access even easier. But for now, keep in mind that only a small portion of the world's rich scholarly knowledge is available in electronic format. An Internet search may help you determine the books and journals that will be needed for your course work, but you will still have to rely on other means to bring print materials to you or travel to where you can get them. If you want to be successful in your program, don't settle for less than access to *all* the resources and services you need from your home institution's library. As you research your program, you may find that the faculty and librarians have collaborated on the online course design. Often library resources are linked right into the course through the course management system used by the faculty member to teach online.

TIP	Ask for References

When inquiring about a program, ask for the names of two or three people who are well along in the program or have recently completed it. Institutions usually have a list of people who have agreed to talk with prospective students. Find out firsthand whether library services were sufficient for their work. An institution may have an attractive website, but that does not mean its services are tried-and-true. Supporting remote access requires good technology that has been adjusted to fit the needs of the students and a knowledgeable staff who can be reached in times of need.

TODAY'S LIBRARIES

The library has always been the student's friend. Whether you have a good library nearby or need to conduct all of your library work online, it's helpful to know some of the basics about these institutions and the people who work there. So, where do you start?

The first place you should conduct your investigation is the library of the institution that's offering the distance education program. We'll call this your "home" library. We strongly recommend that you investigate the library resources available to you from the home institution before you enroll in the program. A clear set of directions and lists of resources aimed at distance learners suggests that significant thought has gone into ensuring good library support for your program. Visit the library's website. Most libraries that support distance learning programs at their institutions have a special Web page that presents information about specialized library support. Look for information on how to find books and print materials, and to access databases. Investigate any of the links you find to special websites that the librarians have assembled as part of the resources they consider important to their patrons. You will also find helpful information about loan policies and remote access to licensed databases, including instructions on how to log into these from home. Licenses serve to restrict unauthenticated users from accessing the information. You want to be sure that you will have the access rights to databases helpful to you.

Once you have identified the library resources available to you as a student in your selected program, you will find it helpful to know what additional local libraries might be useful. Besides local public libraries, you might have access to libraries of nearby colleges and universities, or perhaps specialized resources such as legal and medical libraries associated with local institutions. A walk through the library listings of local Yellow Pages and government pages in your telephone directory may yield important resources. A few calls to nearby libraries will equip you with basic information such as hours of operation, checkout policies, and photocopy costs. And the home page of most state libraries includes links to all the libraries in the state that are Internet accessible. A link to the state library page is usually available from your state government Web page.

If you are investigating a college or university library, you should find out about the strengths of its book and journal collections. Does it collect materials in the field you wish to study? One way to find out is to look at the course offerings and see if the subject you are interested in is taught there. Check the library Web pages for links that might give details about special collections of materials that might be helpful. Many large college libraries have extensive special collections, sometimes housed in a specific area of the library, or even in a different building. The resources of these special collections are not always listed in the online catalog. In fact, a good question to ask any library is, "Do you have special resources appropriate to my course work but not listed in the online catalog?" You may find out about newly acquired items or treasures for which the library has lacked the resources to make fully public. You will also find that many large universities have a main library plus other specialized libraries around campus. These may have access and loan policies different from those of the main library. Many colleges, universities, and museums are working on digitization projects to make these valuable materials available on the Internet. For example, the Library of Congress and the Smithsonian have many new collections of materials on their websites.

Next we turn to identifying the different types of library services and access to resources that make up good-quality library support: online catalogs, databases, interlibrary loans, and reference help.

THE ELEMENTS OF LIBRARY ACCESS

The Online Catalog

Most library catalogs are now computerized and offer a Web-based user interface to the holdings; the traditional drawers of file cards are almost as antiquated as the chained-book libraries of the sixteenth century. The electronic catalog is more accurate, and listings are more likely to be current. It's easier, faster, and more powerful to use, because you can tailor your search quite precisely. In an online catalog, each book has an electronic record that describes it. The record provides information about the author, title, publisher, date, and subjects covered. In addition, some records include special notes about the material. An online library catalog contains records for far more than the books on the shelves. It contains records for nonprint media such as videos, DVDs, and audio recordings. It may also provide links to some of the journal collections that are online in full-text form, as well as links to electronic books and other types of digital media.

Searching the catalog. Once you are connected to an online library catalog, find out what indexes can be searched. Indexes present no mysteries: You use sets of indexes every time you pick up the phone book. The white pages are an alphabetical index of names. The Yellow Pages are an index of "subjects," of services and products.

An online catalog is also a set of indexes. In the catalogs, you will find index categories such as "Author Search," "Title Search," "Keyword," or "Subject Search." If there are examples of each type of search, look at them for helpful clues on how to search. The subject search may be an index of "controlled headings." These are the authoritative subjects set by, for example, the Library of Congress or the National Library of Medicine. Searching in this type of index may help you establish the correct terminology needed to search precisely and give you related subject headings. When you find a record with a subject heading related to your research, click on it to obtain a list of all records with the same heading.

A keyword index in an online catalog helps search for a word or combination of words in parts of the record. You can begin employing some powerful search tools at this point. These tools will be important in almost all of your online searching. The tools are called *Boolean operators* and are the simple words *and, or,* and *not*. Some databases have additional tools or variations of these basic tools, but these are the most commonly found operators.

The *and* operator narrows your search. An example of this type of search statement would be "volcan* and Oregon." Note the asterisk in *volcan**. This is a helpful little tool that will automatically search the terms *volcano, volcanic, volcanism,* and *volcanology*. Quotation marks enclosing a phrase signify that the words must appear together. Thus, when this search is performed, the records found must have one of the variations of *volcan** and the word *Oregon* in them. The *or* operator broadens your search. An example would be "volcan* and (Oregon or California)." Now your search will pick up records that include the variations of *volcan**, and either of the words *Oregon* or *California* must appear with those variations. The parentheses around the terms *Oregon* and *California* indicate that they cannot appear alone in the record but must have a variation of *volcan** in the record as well.

Narrowing the search. You may have the option of "limiting" your search—that is, adding more "directions" to your search—in order to narrow it and remove unwanted titles. For example, you might choose to limit your search to items in English, or to items published after 1990. Using the limit option may help you to reduce the number of records from hundreds down to a more manageable list of just what you need. Other indexes in the catalog might allow you to search only periodical titles, or video titles.

Searching combined university libraries. Your home institution's library may be a part of a consortium of libraries with a union catalog, which includes the holdings of all the consortium's member libraries. For instance, OhioLink, one of the largest academic library consortia, combines the holdings of more than 84 academic libraries in Ohio and contains more than 39 million items. The Orbis Cascade Alliance catalog allows you to search the combined collections of most colleges and universities in Oregon and Washington. The most amazing part of these two systems and other similar ones is that each has a courier system to transfer the books to the member libraries. You may be able to request a book from any member library in the system and have it in as little as two days. The catch: you will almost certainly have to be currently enrolled in one of the member colleges or universities in order to be allowed to order materials. The websites of some of the major library consortia are listed on the Guide's website.

Why might you need to search such a huge database of titles? You might be researching a very specialized topic or a new topic about which little has been published. Materials that can help you are more likely to appear in such a huge database. Once you have identified the book, journal, or other materials you are looking for, you will probably need to

---

TIP	Check Your Spelling

As you search, remember that spelling is important. If you misspell a word in your search command, the search can turn up empty or provide incorrect information. Although some search engines check entries for typos and spelling errors, you should still get into the habit of rechecking what you have typed.

submit an interlibrary loan request through your local library's interlibrary loan services. Interlibrary loans are discussed in more detail later in the chapter.

Library Databases

Periodical databases often provide the most current research on a topic. These databases allow you to search for journal, magazine, and newspaper articles. Most libraries now have a variety of electronic databases. The library home page will link you to a list of available databases. There may be dozens of database options, and you will need to become familiar with those that will be the most effective for the types of information you wish to find. Often there is an information icon next to the database name. By clicking on this icon, you will receive information about the database. Periodical databases are usually governed by license agreements, which may not allow remote access. License restrictions or technical limitations may not allow certain databases to be networked and made available on multiple computers. Also, library computers may have specially modified hardware or software that facilitates access and printing.

A tour of local libraries will surely be an eye-opening experience. Many libraries have special databases, often on CD-ROM, that may be available only on select computers in the library. Do not assume that every computer in the library is the same or that all have the same databases. Also never assume that access to library databases from home equals that available on-site at the library. Usually you must be a currently enrolled student or employee in order to access licensed databases from off campus. Be creative—by taking an extension course or one regular course, you may get access to resources you can't buy. Always ask when you enroll in a program whether or not library databases will be available to you from off campus. Keep in mind that some distance learning programs have rolling enrollments, and there could be a delay between enrolling and when the data authorizing your access to the database loaded into the library computers. Additionally, some libraries have special corporate accounts. Check at your place of employment to see if it has established any such relationships, and whether it can help provide access for your research.

Database searching techniques.   We have already discussed basic searching and Boolean terms. It is very important that you understand these and then look for the help or search tips links at each database website. Reading these suggestions can help you hone in on exactly what you want very quickly—a savings in time and energy every student appreciates! For example, a search on "AIDS" in a medical database will result in thousands of articles, but searching "AIDS and children and Nigeria" will yield a much more limited set of results, which you can quickly scan to find the most appropriate citations.

Databases have special features such as allowing you to sort by relevance or date. Some let you search only items available in full text in the database. The first page of database websites provides tips, suggestions, help, and search aids. By carefully reviewing a few of these, you'll become a much more powerful searcher and find that you can quickly move between databases and use your skills in any of them. You will also see that we have only indicated the basics here, and that there is much more to developing good search techniques. A little study of these advanced techniques will pay off handsomely not only in time saved, but in the quality of your research.

There are many databases you can access and search free. You can then request delivery of items in any number of ways, from regular mail, to fax, to package delivery or courier services. For example, the database Ingenta provides indexing of more than 27,000 journals and their articles. For a fee, you can order articles directly. Other high-quality resources for legal, business, medical, and newspaper purposes are the Lexis-Nexis databases. Some newspaper and journal websites offer some of their content in full text, but fees are usually required for access to these sites.

Downloading information.   Many databases allow you to read full-text or full-image files. Sometimes this requires special software on your computer. A common reader is Adobe Acrobat, which is a free program widely available. After you have located items of interest, most databases will allow you to email the text to yourself to read at home as long as you have appropriate software.

Interlibrary Loans

A particularly important service—especially if you're a long way from a major library—is the interlibrary loan. When you're shopping for distance education programs, a key question to ask is: "Will your library provide full interlibrary loan service to me, just as it would for on-campus students?"

In spite of all our electronic marvels, most books and journals are still available only in traditional print formats, and an interlibrary loan is the mechanism that enables libraries to find and loan that material, even when they don't own it themselves. Typically, the library that owns the material will ship a book but send photocopies of journal articles.

There are some important fundamentals about this service, the first of which is that when your library borrows material for you, it is responsible for the material and will have to cover its cost if you lose it. Your library, therefore, has a strong interest in your handling the material properly and returning it on time. Late fees and replacement costs for lost items can be expensive. Replacement costs may include a minimum amount, such as $75, the real cost of the material if more than the minimum, and processing fees. It's important to be aware that failure to address these charges could result in loss of library privileges, refusal to allow your enrollment in additional classes, or even the holding of grades or transcripts.

Some smaller libraries are reluctant to provide interlibrary loans because this service consumes scarce time and resources. Once you're assured that interlibrary loans are routine and welcome, the next questions you should ask are as follows:

- How do I order an item? Can requests be sent via email?
- What is the cost? (Interlibrary loans may not be part of a library's free service.)
- How long does it take, and how will I be notified that the material has arrived?
- What is the loan period and are renewals available?

The usual interlibrary loan is from one library to another and then finally to you. You will normally pick up the items you've ordered at the library through which you made your request—your home library. If your request is for a journal article, the library supplying the document may scan it and send it over the Internet to your home library. Your library may allow you to "pick up" your document electronically from your own computer, rather than have you pick it up in person.

When using interlibrary loans, be realistic about your research deadlines: the process of locating, ordering, and delivering your material can take from a few days to several weeks.

What if you are in an area with no interlibrary loan service? Unless the library for your program will order the materials and send them directly to you, you may have to travel to the nearest large town with a good public or college library. You will need a library card, so be sure to ask the library what services the card provides and how long the card is valid. Many libraries offer cards to those outside their service areas for a fee. Costs can vary from as little as $10 to more than $100. College and university libraries may have more restrictive access policies than public libraries, and few, if any, will allow you to use interlibrary loan services if you are not an enrolled student.

Reference Help

If you intend to use library services extensively, get to know the people working in reference, circulation, and interlibrary loan. Whom should you talk to at a library to get the most informed service? During many hours of the day, students or part-time employees may staff the circulation or checkout desk. They generally receive some training, but if they can't answer your questions with assurance, try the reference desk. Reference librarians will know how to acquire special services and even something about special agreements with other libraries and colleges that may be helpful to you. If the library has a home page, see if it has a department/staff directory with phone numbers and possibly email addresses.

Librarians like to help. As with most jobs, the more uncommon the problem, the more interesting it becomes. Think about what you need help finding—statistics? books? journal articles? maps? video or audio materials? Every library is different. Most buy certain core reference materials such as general encyclopedias; some have special collections in specific areas; and some are depositories for local, state, or federal documents. If you have access to several libraries, do some research to determine which one has the best resources for you.

TIP | **Avoid Library Rush Hours**

To get more help with complex questions, find out the times when the library is least busy—typically in the early morning or dinner hours. At college libraries, remember that many students do their research midterm (or at the last possible moment), inundating the library with special requests. If you can, schedule your research visits during quieter periods, perhaps calling for an appointment with a reference librarian. Service might be especially good between terms, because many college libraries remain open even when classes are not in session. Be sure to ask about services and hours of operation between terms.

Smaller public and academic libraries are not equipped to provide the resources of a research university library, but if you plan your work carefully, they can help you locate materials and borrow what is needed from other libraries. Your local library, no matter how large or small, wants to help. Take time to know the resources and the staff. The payoff will be shorter time lines and lower costs as you do your research.

For those of you lacking access to good libraries, the Internet does offer other options. You can order books online, for example, from Amazon.com or Barnesnoble.com. Some books no longer under copyright restrictions are available online at no cost. And there is a commercial site called NetLibrary for access to electronic books. For a fee, you can "check out" electronic titles. Our companion website has links to many sources. Try, for example, "Best Information on the Net," which in turn will steer you to many useful resources.

WHAT SERVICES ARE AVAILABLE AND HOW EFFECTIVE ARE THEY?

Keep in mind that although you may be taking a course from a very distant college, you probably need the same library service as the students who are on campus. When you're considering a college, university, or other institution offering courses at a distance, you need to know that its library—or a very good substitute—will be there for you, wherever you are and whenever you need it. Fortunately, an increasing number of libraries provide good service at a distance.

How do you judge whether a college or a given library can offer you the service you'll need? Possible services range from an electronic "reserve book room," ready to deliver online the material your instructor prescribes for your course, to more limited service that is restricted to people who can do their work within the library walls. Some libraries will fax documents or provide special shipping arrangements on request. They may need to charge for some of these services, so you'll want to check your options. Document delivery systems that speed the transfer of scanned documents over the Internet are also being used by some libraries. Sometimes these systems allow delivery directly to the student through email. The type of hardware and software you have may limit the quality of the transfer, so be sure to check with the interlibrary loan office about this option. As mentioned earlier, these files often require a program such as Adobe Acrobat in order to read them. One measure of quality service: when you call the library at the institution offering your program, an easily reachable person who is knowledgeable about distance education should be there to help.

Evaluating databases. Most libraries subscribe to various electronic databases. Evaluating them can be complicated, because there are major differences in what these databases index, how well they handle complex searches, how much full text is available, and how easy they are to use.

Questions to Ask Librarians Concerning Helpful Databases

1. How many publications does this database index?
2. What percentage are available full text or full image? (For an explanation of full text and full image, see the section "Specialized Databases" later in this chapter.)
3. What publications in my field of study are represented in this database?
4. How many of these titles are available full text or full image?
5. How far back are these titles indexed?

Consider one prominent example. The Online Computer Library Center, Inc. (universally known by its initials, OCLC) has a product called FirstSearch. It provides access to more than 100 databases in many disciplines. Some of the databases have full text online. FirstSearch allows you to order the article and have it sent by fax or regular U.S. mail if you have an account. Many public and academic libraries offer FirstSearch to their users. Ask the reference or information desk about this service.

Other major database vendors include Ebsco, LexisNexis, Ovid, and ProQuest. Each offers many databases. A reference librarian can help you select which databases are best for your field, subject, or research topic.

If you have no access to databases like these, you are at a severe disadvantage in comparison with on-campus students.

Evaluating library service. To what extent can you expect high-quality library service from the institution providing your distance education program? How much can you rely on local libraries to supply you with needed resources? These are areas of supreme importance if you are interested in quality education. You should have the answers to some serious questions and be comfortable with your options before you pay for the courses.

Questions to Ask Distance Education Providers About Library Services

1 *Is there a librarian who works with distance education students?*

2 *How do I get a computer account in order to access the institution's email and database services?*

3 *What interlibrary loan services are available?*

- How quickly are items delivered?
- Where are the items delivered? Can they be shipped directly to me?

4 *What reference desk services are available?*

- Who answers questions, and can I use email, telephone, or fax?
- Is the telephone number toll free?
- How quickly are email or faxed questions answered?

5 *Is an orientation to the library services offered?*

6 *Are there special online resources available to me if I enroll in the provider's program?*

7 *Are there arrangements with local libraries so that I can use them as "extensions" of the provider's library?*

You should consider a different distance education provider if you cannot get good answers to these questions in a timely manner.

USING THE INTERNET AND THE WORLD WIDE WEB

You have identified the resources available to you through the institution providing your distance education program, or through your local public or college libraries, but there are other possibilities. What is available to you on the Internet? Once you are equipped with the hardware and software discussed in Chapter 3, sitting in front of a computer connected to the Internet, browser at the ready, where do you go? How do you know that what you find is authoritative and not propaganda? How can you know whether you've found the best information available? How do you get access to important databases that charge a fee?

You should first know about some myths of online information. Some people seem to believe that all information is available somewhere on the World Wide Web. Not so. Another myth is that everything on the Internet is free. Hardly. Sometimes portions of commercial copyrighted material may appear, but often it is there to entice you to go out and purchase the complete version. Many information sites have home pages, but to access and search the data, you will need an account or subscription. Another common misperception is that search engines find everything on the Internet on your topic. Actually, they locate only a small percentage and they use different methods for judging relevance. Certainly all that is out there is not reliable. An editorial in one leading medical journal, the *Journal of the American Medical Association*, commented:

> The problem is not too little information but too much, vast chunks of it incomplete, misleading, or inaccurate, and not only in the medical area. The Net—and especially the Web—has the potential to become the world's largest vanity press. It is a medium in which anyone with a computer can serve simultaneously as author, editor, and publisher and can fill any or all of those roles anonymously if he or she so chooses. In such an environment, novices and savvy Internet users alike can have trouble distinguishing the wheat from the chaff, the useful from the harmful.*

Yes indeed! There are websites based on everything from rumor and innuendo to outright fantasy, with all the information seemingly accurate and reliable. Some cues to quality control are described later.

Searching the Internet. You can use the Internet to search virtually any topic or issue. You may have a known website to visit, but most of the time you will want to find out what's available about the subject at hand. There are two different ways to approach searching for information on the World Wide Web: looking through directories and using search engines. Some sites blend the two and even offer something called "metasearching," a method for searching multiple search engines. Web resources are, to say the least, dynamic: new stars appear and old friends fade away. You will find an up-to-date guide with hyperlinks to many of the best current resources—including those mentioned in this chapter—at the website that accompanies this Guide. Have your password handy when you log on. We want to emphasize that it's wise to begin at your home library and look for a link to "Web Resources" or something similar. Librarians have assembled good

---

* "Assessing, controlling, and assuring the quality of medical information on the Internet: *caveat lector et viewor*—let the reader and viewer beware." Editorial, William A. Silberg, George D. Lundberg, and Robert Musacchio, *Journal of the American Medical Association*, 1997; 277 (15): 1244.

sites and often have categorized them in helpful ways to allow easy ways to find great resources. Additionally, the following sections provide some good places to start.

Directories and libraries. A good first stop is the structured directory in Yahoo! By following its directories to narrower and narrower areas or topics, you can arrive at a list of resources on the Internet, all directly related to a topic or subject area. The Librarians' Index to the Internet is another example of a good directory.

Some directories of Web pages offer sites carefully selected according to some criteria for inclusion. Many library home pages offer links to special resources grouped by subject. Try, for example, The Internet Public Library. It's another good attempt by librarians to bring some order to the Internet.

You can connect to several other important sources via our website. Here are some examples:

- Infomine and AcademicInfo are good comprehensive directories for scholarly research on the Web.
- Refdesk.com offers many useful links that are regularly checked.
- Martindale's The Reference Desk provides particularly good science links.
- Best Information on the Net is a fine collection of sites from St. Ambrose University's librarians. It has an electronic reading room and links to full-text sites and online bookstores.
- And recall the earlier references to the online catalogs of libraries and library consortia, including those of the University of California at the California Digital Library site, Ohiolink, and many hundreds you can find by searching university and college websites.

Search engines. Along with Internet directories and library reference sources, you can locate information by using one of the search engines available on the Internet. These engines have different features, and they search different parts of the Internet. It's a good idea to review some of the comparisons of search engines available in print and on the Internet. First, you should know the basic principles common to most of the engines. Then you will know how to structure your search to retrieve the best available information for your work.

Some search engine basics. We've covered search basics for online catalogs and electronic databases, but most search engines have some special features and they search and deliver results differently. It is helpful to know these basics about Boolean operators, and using parentheses or quotation marks to group search words to search together in that order so you can create good searches. Constructing a solid search depends on two things: the features of the search engine and your ability to work with the terms you want to search. The best way to learn is to try some searches, read the help pages offered on the home pages of the search engines, and look at some of the sites listed below. This will help you understand the power and limitations of the search engines. We have mentioned only a few basic search techniques here. Each search engine will have tips and help—as with the databases, these are worth reading. Also, your home library may include tutorials on searching techniques on its Web pages. If not, look at the well-researched guides found easily at the library pages for the University of California, Berkeley.

WARNING! Searching is fun, but effective searching is not easy. You will need to learn how to construct a search and how the different search engines work. Plan to try three or four different engines. Practice some searches on them until you're confident that you can quickly compose an effective search. Here are some highly rated search engines:

- AlltheWeb Advanced has very powerful advanced searching options.
- Teoma ranks sites by what it calls "subject specific popularity."
- AltaVista is one of the largest and allows Boolean searching in the advanced mode.
- Google often wins high honors and has a nice feature that checks your entry for typos and spelling errors.
- Yahoo! has links to all types of searching tools for the Internet. It is both a directory and search engine.
- Vivisimo is called a metasearch engine because it uses your terms to simultaneously search multiple search engines. It returns results clustered in hierarchical categories. For instance, a search on "redwood forest ecology" clusters results under "Watershed," "Ecosystems," "Botany-Coastal Redwoods," "Logging," and several more categories.

Specialized databases.   There are special databases on the Internet where you can perform detailed searches for specific information. You can find many of these databases listed at the site of the University of California at Berkeley. Particularly valuable for medical research is Medline; most American medical journals are indexed here, and many important foreign journals are included. Searching is free.

Ingenta, mentioned earlier, is an all-purpose database for journal article citations on any number of topics. It indexes millions of articles from more than 5,000 online publications. Scirus is a "science-specific" engine that searches free sites and the journal databases. Before paying for quick-service full-text delivery of journal articles, find out if the journal is available at one of your local libraries or through interlibrary loan.

In searching journal databases, be aware that the content may be just citations and abstracts, or it may be entire articles. Full-text articles usually include the text but no pictures, graphs, charts, or illustrations of any kind. Full-image articles, however, generally appear as they do in print. Such documents may be downloaded, but they may require a special reader program such as Adobe Acrobat. This reader program is available free for almost every type of computer at many places on the Internet.

Sometimes subscribing to a newspaper, magazine, or journal gets you privileged electronic access through the use of a password. You might find it cost-effective to subscribe to one or more of these publications in order to get access to their databases. Often you can search back issues or obtain access to special information only available to subscribers. Also check with your librarian to learn if the library subscribes. If it does, the librarian can do Web searches for you (libraries don't usually give out the password). Important resources such as the *Wall Street Journal* and the *New York Times* provide password access.

Internet training. There are classes that teach Internet searching. Your local library or college may offer some. Sometimes you can find library courses and tutorials online. Earlier we mentioned a website managed by the library faculty at the University of California, Berkeley, that is designed to teach effective Internet search strategies. The site is regularly updated with the latest teaching tips direct from classroom testing. There are links to all the search engines, but, more important, there are instructions for how to—and how not to—search. Specific directions are included to guide you in constructing searches in the major engines and metasearch engines. Instructions for effectively investigating directories such as Yahoo! can be found here also. Beyond General World Wide Web Searching has links to Virtual Reference Libraries and Full-Text Resource Locators. There is also a good guide on how to cite Internet resources. InfoPeople is a website that maintains easy-to-read and excellent search engine information, including charts comparing search engine features.

Useful library skills courses are available on the Web, complete with lessons and assignments. You can link there directly from our site. The lessons cover Internet searching, common databases, and many helpful tips on using libraries.

Determining the quality of what you find.   You've located some information, but how reliable is it? Is it authoritative, unbiased, and backed up with solid evidence? What are some useful criteria for evaluating sites? You can begin with some of the qualifiers you would use for a print source:

- Who is the author?
- What are the author's credentials?
- Is the author affiliated with an institution?
- Does the author document his or her sources?
- What evidence is brought to support the information?
- If statistics are cited, are the sources provided?
- How current is the material and when was the site last updated?
- What's the nature of the site? You can determine whether it's associated with government, education, an organization, or a commercial company by looking for .gov, .edu, .org, or .com in the site address.

You can use the Internet to find out more about an author and the institutions with which he or she may be affiliated by searching for the author's home pages or using a search engine to locate publications. Especially in the sciences, recent publications may appear on the Internet. Searching a journal citation index such as Ingenta might reveal other publications by the author.

The information on your distance learning provider's website should be considered accurate. Most of the information on educational institutions' academic "official" pages is accurate. But beware: Most educational institutions provide space for "personal" pages for faculty, staff, and students. So the Web page you're looking at from that prestigious university may have been put up by a student who, with good intentions, has "published" inaccurate information. Even faculty personal pages may be an expression of an individual's personal thoughts or beliefs and may not be generally accepted in his or her profession. Commercial and organizational sites can be similarly misleading.

The website associated with *Seaching and Researching on the Internet and the World Wide Web,* a book by Ernest Ackermann and Karen Hartman (Wilsonville, OR: Franklin, Beedle & Associates) includes a good glossary and links to helpful information on using the Internet and the Web. You can link to it directly from our website.

SUMMARY: QUESTIONS AND CHOICES

As you choose a distance learning program, an obvious question is "Can I really take the courses from where I am?" More often than not, an important part of that question is: "How can I get the library services that I'll need?"

Some courses are essentially self-contained, with all the necessary material provided and no need for library support. Most, however, require some independent digging for information, and for that, you'll need a library that can supply what you need, when you need it, with no more out-of-pocket cost than necessary.

In this chapter, we've examined your prospective options and some of the pertinent questions. In summary, it may be helpful to review some of the most important issues:

1. I'm considering a distance education program from College X.
   - Can I access the college library's catalog online?
   - Can I have online access to the same electronic resources that are available to students who visit the library?
   - Are reference librarians available to me? May I send questions and requests by phone, email, or fax? What's the likely response time to an email or fax request?
   - Will the college library ship material to me?

- Is there an electronic reserve reading room for my prospective course? Can I access it from here, with the hardware and software that are available to me?
- Will the college library get material for me by interlibrary loan? If so, how will I receive the material? How long will it take? Will there be any cost?
- Will the course material be available in a nearby learning center affiliated with the college?
- Is there a distance education librarian available to help?

2. If College X's library can't provide these services, is another option available, such as a nearby public library or another academic library? What services can it provide? Are these services appropriate for my program? What would they cost?

3. To what extent might Internet searches fulfill my library requirements? How would I get access to the databases I need, and at what cost?

Such a list of questions may seem daunting, but you don't want to be blindsided—you don't want to register for a program and then find that you can't get the books, documents, or online information that you need. Remember the old saw "Better safe than sorry." In fact, the institutions that offer the best distance education programs have good answers to these questions, and you'll find that a rapidly increasing number of libraries are prepared to provide the services you need.

As we said at the beginning of this chapter, today's library is a major key to the information age, and today's librarians may be the distance learner's best friends.

 www.DLGuide.info
Visit this website for additional information and activities.

CHAPTER 5

UNDERSTANDING YOUR NEEDS

Overcoming the Personal Barriers to Success in Distance Learning

In this chapter, you will

- ◆ learn to clarify your goals for being a student and participating in distance learning
- ◆ learn to understand your attitudes toward distance learning
- ◆ discover how to prioritize your roles and responsibilities so that being a student is high on the list
- ◆ find ways to identify and develop academic and social support systems within your distance learning courses
- ◆ identify questions to ask and resources to explore if you have a disability that requires special accommodation
- ◆ learn to value health as important to goal achievement and course success

Students who succeed in distance learning are able to focus on their goals, prioritize their responsibilities, reach out for the assistance they need, and pay attention to their health. This chapter is designed to help you develop the skills of other successful distance learners.

LEARNING FROM OTHERS

You know the old saying, "Hindsight is 20/20." Scattered throughout this chapter are stories and "sidebars of advice" obtained from the experiences of distance learners. Their purpose is to let you learn from the hindsight of others who have attempted and succeeded in distance learning. These anecdotes should provide you with information about how to succeed and some perspective on how to handle the personal challenges of being a college student at a distance.

WHERE TO LEARN MORE

There are a number of resources to pursue if you wish to explore in more detail any of the topics covered in this chapter. These resources include both print and nonprint information and, for the most part, are just the tip of the iceberg. A selected resource listing will be updated regularly on the Guide's companion website.

TIP	Advice from Other Distance Learners

When asked what advice they would give to others who are about to participate in distance learning, students in a variety of undergraduate and graduate television classes had the following responses:

- Be committed—give it all you have!
- Participate—ask questions—pay attention.
- Be familiar with a computer.
- Form a "buddy system" or small groups to support each other.
- Be prepared to work independently.

CLARIFYING YOUR GOALS AND ATTITUDES

Students who don't have at least some idea why they are in college are more likely to drop out or find themselves in academic difficulty. So, it's important that you have at least a preliminary goal for taking college courses and, in particular, distance learning courses. Asking yourself three basic questions will help you clarify your goals and attitudes:

1. Why do I want to be a student?
2. Why do I want to participate in distance learning?
3. What are my attitudes toward distance learning?

Why Do You Want to Be a Student?

There are a variety of reasons people give for being a student, such as the following:

- to help in a current job
- to move toward a new job or career change
- to move toward a college degree and a career
- to have the ability to do a particular job (e.g., licensing issues)
- because friends are students
- because it's the thing to do after high school
- to learn about a particular topic (personal enrichment)

These reasons reflect the *value* that people place on the importance of being a student. For example, if you need college courses to be able to keep your job, being a student will have a different value (and priority) than if you don't need them and you have no particular need or desire for a degree. *What are your reasons for being a student?* Answer in the space provided or use Worksheet #1 on our website.

_____

_____

Why Do You Want to Participate in Distance Learning?

There are many and varied reasons for choosing distance learning. Here are some of the more common ones:

- to save on travel time
- because it is convenient to my schedule

- to fulfill a desire to try a new learning situation
- because of a preference to learn independently
- because the topic/content being offered is of interest
- because the content isn't offered in a traditional, campus-based setting
- because attending campus classes isn't possible

How about you? *Why are you interested in distance learning*? Answer in the space provided or use Worksheet #1 on our website.

_____

_____

What Are Your Attitudes Toward Distance Learning?

Attitudes toward course content affect your interest in and approach to learning (e.g., the "math-phobic" person). Attitudes toward course delivery systems can also affect your interest in, approach to, and success in learning. Does your reason for participating in distance learning influence your motivation to learn? If so, how? For example, if your preference is to take courses in a traditional, campus-based classroom setting but the course you want or need is not offered in that form, how will this affect your interest and motivation to learn? *What are your attitudes toward distance learning?* Answer in the space provided or use Worksheet #1 on our website.

_____

_____

Putting It Together

Worksheet #1, "Clarifying Your Goals and Attitudes" (see the website) has been designed for you to record your answers to the three basic questions. Your answers to the first two questions will be useful in setting your priorities. The responses you give regarding your attitudes toward distance learning may require further action on your part. For example, if you are quite skeptical about distance learning, review Chapter 1. Sometimes people are skeptical because they don't have enough information. If after learning more about distance learning you remain skeptical, determine whether the concerns you have will interfere with your learning in the course. If they will, perhaps dis-

TIP	Advice from One Distance Learner

Be aware that if you are not willing to use time management and set priorities, distance learning is not going to work for you. You are making a commitment. Be aware that you will need to make lifestyle choices.

tance learning is not the mode for you. Remember that you know yourself better than anyone! *Being honest in your assessment is the best way to ensure your success!*

THE ESSENCE OF BEING HUMAN: TOO MANY ROLES, TOO LITTLE TIME

Successful distance learners are able to prioritize their commitments effectively. This involves understanding and juggling the multiple roles we play as human beings. For many of us, these are almost impossible tasks.

Being human in modern society means that we find ourselves wearing many different "hats." In sociology, these hats are referred to as *roles*. Roles are often thought of in terms of title or position (e.g., mother, engineer, vice president, Little League coach). We use such terms daily to describe others and ourselves. As each of us assumes a new role, we usually assume the responsibilities and expected actions that *we think are necessary* to be successful in this new role.

Think about yourself in the role of worker. What do you expect of yourself? What behaviors or actions do you need to perform in order to be considered, by yourself and perhaps others, an effective worker? You can ask yourself the same questions about any role. What you will quickly find, and perhaps be surprised by, is that you play many different roles in your life, that each role carries with it a set of expectations regarding behavior, and that some roles have a more significant priority than others do.

For example, you may be an employee for some organization and also be a parent, a spouse, a friend, a brother, or a volunteer. Since you are reading this Guide, you are also currently or potentially a *student*. Given all your roles, you already know that it is difficult to accomplish everything you need and want to do within the time you have to do it. How can you possibly take on anything else, especially something that takes as much time as being a student?

From Chaos to Order: Determining Opportunity Costs

To bring order to the chaos of our lives, and to make room for new roles, such as that of student, we need to acknowledge the various roles we play and make decisions about each role's importance to us. In essence, we need to *prioritize*. Prioritizing is a critical process as you take on the role of student and even more important when you are a student learning at a distance. Unfortunately, prioritizing roles tends to be a process done more informally than formally without considering the consequences of the actions. As harsh as it sounds and sometimes is, taking on the role of student may mean that you have to give up, or at least temporarily postpone, something else. Remember—you're prioritizing in anticipation of some reward in the end, such as course completion, a college degree, or a job promotion.

Making decisions about priorities requires you to determine the value of adding the role of student to your life and weighing it against the value of what you will have to give up or postpone in order to take on that role. The basic question for you to ask yourself is, *"Is taking on the role of student worth it to me—and why?"*

Avoiding Murphy's Law: Prioritizing and Negotiating Role Commitments and Responsibilities

Most likely, the role commitments that will interfere with your courses fall into the "work" and "family" categories. This certainly makes sense given that these roles are often viewed as the most important and the most difficult to postpone because the demands are often beyond your own control.

According to Murphy's Law, something can and will go awry during your distance learning course. However, this shouldn't stop you from pursuing distance learning. By prioritizing and negotiating with significant others you can increase your capacity to overcome any crisis and help ensure your success as a learner.

TIP	Advice from One Distance Learner

To ensure your success, the role of student needs to have value to you and to occupy a high priority in your life.

In setting your priorities to incorporate the role of student, refer back to your answers about why you want to be a student and why you want to participate in distance learning. Then, applying the priority-setting process outlined in the next few pages, answer the following question: *"How important is being a student compared to your other roles and responsibilities?"*

This evaluation is essential if you are to successfully manage your time and maneuver around any crisis that may occur. Goal setting and priority setting are critical parts of your plan for educational success. All too often people neglect these processes because they think they can handle anything that comes their way. Foresight and forethought are *always* better than hindsight in the case of college success.

Priority Setting as Life Management

Sometimes the process of setting priorities is considered a form of time management. Although prioritizing your roles and responsibilities can be considered the first step in the development of a more day-to-day or weekly time management plan, it is also a form of *life management*.

Before you begin to map out a detailed daily or weekly time management plan, you should decide whether you are ready and able to take the class or classes in the first place. This involves determining your role commitments, prioritizing them according to their value or importance to you, and determining the amount of time you need to devote to them each week. There are many different systems you can use, some of which are included in the resources for this chapter. What follows next is a quick and simple approach to making decisions about your role priorities.

Three Steps to Setting Your Priorities

In prioritizing your roles, you need to

1. list the major roles you play.
2. rate the importance of each role to you using a simple rating scale.
3. determine how much time you will spend each week engaged in each role activity.

The amount of time you spend on a role priority should coincide with the importance of that priority to you. Worksheets #2 and #3 were developed to help you understand your roles and priorities—with and without the role of student. Copies of these worksheets can be downloaded from our website.

To show you how easy, yet important, understanding your roles and priorities is to your academic success, here is an example of how one student engaged in this process. By working through the worksheets, Cheryl is able to identify what is truly important to her and what she felt she could and could not "give up" in order to take her course successfully.

A Process in Action: Cheryl's Experience

Cheryl is a married professional woman with a 10-month-old child. Her husband is also a professional and both devote 50–60 hours per week to their jobs, which happen to be with the same company. Daycare is provided on site, and their child is enrolled, so there are opportunities for each of them to visit during the day. Cheryl decides that she really needs to explore a different career field that will allow her to spend more time with their child. As a family, they have become accustomed to a particular lifestyle, so a major salary reduction is not possible but a slight reduction will be okay. Cheryl and her husband make a joint decision that she should explore other career options. Cheryl decides to "test the waters" by taking a college course that will move her in a new direction. The course she wishes to take is a late evening course. The course description indicates that there is much independent work as well as a required group project. No one in the class lives closer than a 30-minute drive from the site, with many living as far away as a 60-minute drive. Participating in the course will mean that Cheryl will be away from home at least one evening a week (her job also requires her to be away from home at times) and that she will have to devote time to doing the course assignments. Given a more than full-time job and her family responsibilities, Cheryl needs to set some priorities. Here's how she completes Worksheet #2:

Cheryl's Worksheet #2
Understanding Your Roles and Priorities
(without the role of student)

Role	Perceived Priority (rate in order of importance with 1 being the most important)					Time Spent on Activity Each Week
	1	2	3	4	5	
Work (manager, employee)	X	—	—	—	—	60
Family (parent & wife)	X	—	—	—	—	42
Friends/Social	—	X	—	—	—	6
Leisure (reading, watching TV)	—	X	—	—	—	10
Other						
Volunteer	—	—	X	—	—	2
	—	—	—	—	—	—
	—	—	—	—	—	—

Subtotal time	120
Add hours you sleep	+ 48*
Total time	168

*Includes naps with child.

With all of her time accounted for in these roles, it is clear to Cheryl that changes must be made so she can be successful in taking her class. Through discussions with her husband, they renegotiate the time each spends with their child. At work, through task delegation, Cheryl is able to reduce her work schedule by five hours per week. She also decides that her role as a volunteer will have to be put on hold for at least this semester. Reducing sleep and leisure time is not an option for Cheryl. The time allotted for sleep includes the minimum amount needed for her to feel rested (six hours per night) plus the amount she devotes to getting her child to sleep. Her leisure time allows her to unwind and, because it is already minimal, not viewed as something that can be reduced. As a couple, Cheryl and her husband also agree to temporarily cut back on their weekend get-togethers with their friends from two to three times a month to no more than twice. These reordered priorities provide Cheryl with the time she needs to do her course work and enable her to accommodate an unexpected crisis such as if a family member becomes seriously ill. She contributes to her group assignments, through email as well as fax, and she achieves an A in the course. Cheryl's reordered priorities are reflected in Worksheet #3:

Cheryl's Worksheet #3

Building the Role of Student into Your Roles and Priorities

Role	Perceived Priority (rate in order of importance with 1 being the most important)					Time Spent on Activity Each Week
	1	2	3	4	5	
Work (manager, employee)	X	—	—	—	—	55
Family (parent & wife)	X	—	—	—	—	32
Friends/Social	—	X	—	—	—	4
Leisure (reading, watching TV)	—	X	—	—	—	10
Other						
Student	X	—	—	—	—	19*
	—	—	—	—	—	—
	—	—	—	—	—	—

Subtotal time	120
Add hours you sleep	+ 48[†]
Total time	168

*Includes travel time.
[†]Includes naps with child.

As you can see, by carefully negotiating her various roles and priorities, Cheryl was able to meet her responsibilities and successfully complete her course, achieving the highest grade possible. This can be possible for you, too. Try completing the worksheets yourself. A couple of general guidelines should help you:

- Remember that there are *only* 168 hours in a week.
- As a general rule of thumb for anticipating how much time a college course will take, equate one three-credit course to about 10 hours per week. This includes time in formal instruction (if there is any) and study time. Not all courses fit this guideline, but it is a good place to start.

Listed next are the questions asked throughout this section and a few more to help you make your decisions about distance learning.

- What are your reasons for being a student?
- Why do you want to participate in distance learning?
- What are your attitudes toward distance learning?
- What roles do you currently play and how do they rate in importance in relationship to one another?
- How important is being a student compared to your other roles and responsibilities?
- What role priorities can be adjusted to accommodate your student role? Taking distance learning courses requires more independent learning. How do you plan to adjust them? What role priorities are absolute and cannot be changed? What roles can be adjusted with acceptable consequences? Additional questions to ask yourself as you evaluate and prioritize your roles include the following:
  - How much time will you spend working? Is this required or your personal preference?
  - How much sleep do you require to be at your best?
  - Are you a morning, afternoon, or evening person? In other words, when are you at your best for learning? Knowing this will help you decide when it is best to take courses.
  - What about your leisure time and social life? How can you make sure that you preserve at least some of these positive activities?

- What situations do you anticipate may pose problems for you during the course of your distance learning experience, such as family illness, job changes, or relocation? It is important to consider these possible events and how you will deal with them if they occur. Remember—foresight and forethought are the keys to a successful college experience.

A little preplanning can go a long way to bolster your motivation and commitment to pursuing distance learning. The exercises, advice, and examples offered here are designed to help you understand quickly the importance of clarifying goals and prioritizing roles as well as provide you with an easy way to implement these processes for yourself.

DEVELOPING SYSTEMS OF ACADEMIC AND SOCIAL SUPPORT

Much attention has been given to goal and priority setting as a way to help ensure your distance learning success because it is an important process. However, there are other areas of importance to you in your role as student. For example, being able to connect with faculty members, other students, and academic support, such as tutoring, is very important to many distance learners. Once you've committed to a distance learning course, how do you go about connecting with others when learning at a distance? If you find you need academic assistance, how do you go about getting it? If you have a disability that requires accommodation, what questions should you ask to guide you through the process of disclosure, documentation, and accommodation?

In a traditional college course that meets routinely and in which students and faculty are in the same room, classroom interaction or the potential for interaction is always present. It is also somewhat easier for those who routinely travel to a campus to take advantage of the learning resources that might be available. The potential for interaction and connection may not be as easy when the course is offered through distance learning. When contact with faculty members, other students, or campus resources is either limited or nonexistent, you need to be assertive and creative in finding ways to interact and connect to support your learning. What follows are suggestions for initiating and developing systems of academic and social support to meet your needs as a distance learner.

TIP	Use the Buddy System

Make sure you know someone in the class with whom you can brainstorm, discuss problems, and so forth. Try to implement a buddy system.

Connecting and Communicating with Other Students and Faculty Members

If one of the reasons you chose distance learning is the independence of the learning situation, having contact with other students and faculty members may not be an issue. For many students, however, this interaction is important and is positively linked to their academic success. So, it is important to make it possible for distance learners to connect with faculty members and other students either routinely or on an as-needed basis.

Creating Your Own "Community of Learners"

There are a number of ways to create a team of learners to support you in your distance learning courses. In fact, some of these ways, for example, the use of technologies such as Blackboard™ through which students gain access to course materials, communicate with the instructor, and converse with each other, may be "built in" to the structure of your distance learning course. A few other more obvious ways to create a "community of learners" are listed here. For additional information, particularly about those possibilities that involve technology, refer back to Chapter 3.

Sharing students' and faculty members' names, addresses, phone numbers, and email addresses. Ask the instructor teaching the course to distribute a list of his or her name, address, phone number, and email address as well as those of the students taking the course. The instructor will, of course, need to get permission directly from the students in order to give out their contact information.

Getting email addresses. Ask the instructor or the host institution about email addresses. Are you eligible to receive an email address through the institution? How do you get one? If you already have one, can you use it on the institution's system? The use of email will make it easier for you to connect with your instructor and other students in your class.

Using Listservs.   Sometimes faculty members have special computer-based Listservs created for courses. They use these as a way to communicate by email with their students and to respond to individual questions and concerns. Ask your instructor whether there will be a Listserv and, if not, to consider it as a way for students to interact easily with him or her and the other students.

Creating geographically based study groups.   Through a sharing of names and addresses, and by using a Listserv, subgroups of students can be identified who can emerge as learning communities. For example, if you find that a few other students taking the same course as you all live within a reasonable commuting distance, you may be able to create a study support group. Your contact could be face-to-face or through email.

Establishing feedback networks.   You may not want or be able to meet regularly with other students. Telephones and regular mail remain useful tools to help you to establish connections and feedback from others in your distance learning courses.

Sharon's story addresses how she developed her priorities and juggled her multiple roles. It also stresses how essential it was to her to connect with other students and faculty members.

Connecting with Learning Resources and Support

Even the best students may need help with course content from time to time. As a distance learner, you may have to be a little creative in finding ways to facilitate getting the help you need. This section offers some possibilities and questions for you to explore to help you get the help you might need.

First, review your own study habits, using the information in Chapter 6. Are you approaching the study of the material in a way that will help you understand it and reinforce your long-term memory? Those who regularly work with students in the area of academic assistance often find that many students don't require content support. They just need to evaluate and adjust their study habits and/or weekly time management plan.

Second, if you find that you do need assistance with understanding the content and/or concepts of a course, find out what possibilities exist for you. Your instructor may be able to guide you to resources that will help you. Asking your instructor for assistance is important! If you are having difficulty, other students may be having trouble as well. If

A Process in Action

The Development of Academic Support Through Feedback

Sharon is a married, professional woman with two children in college. She is working on a graduate degree and is taking two courses in addition to working full-time. Sharon and her husband have gone through many negotiations regarding roles and responsibilities over the years. Indeed, she believes that having a solid base of family support and sharing of responsibilities is essential to succeeding in college and, in particular, distance learning.

Sharon pursued her undergraduate degree while her children were young and found that it was extremely difficult trying to do everything that needed to be done *and* spend time with her family. The highest priority for Sharon was her family and she found that the adjustments she made in her role priorities were in the areas related to her own leisure activities. The same has been true for her graduate work. Consequently, she sometimes feels as if she is "burning the candle at both ends" and is exhausted by the end of a term. To help get her through each term, she keeps repeating to herself, "It's only for a short time."

Not unlike many distance learners, Sharon found taking a course through distance learning to be convenient to her schedule. The trade-off in time more than made up for the lack of face-to-face interaction that she experienced in her undergraduate and some of her graduate courses. The most recent distance learning course she took was a television course at a receive site at the elementary school in her hometown. One other person was at this site.

Sharon did well in the course and believes that support, particularly in the form of feedback, is very important in letting students know how well they are doing. She found that although her instructor did distribute the names and addresses of all students taking the course at all locations, she relied mostly on the other person at the site for support when she needed it. The two of them were able to discuss issues and provide some feedback, which, because of the large number of students taking the class, at times seemed slow in coming from the instructor.

TIP	Success with Course Content

- Be very involved in the class.
- Stay on top of the work.
- Ask questions if you don't understand.

you don't voice your concerns and need for assistance, your instructor may never know there is a problem. Ask your instructor the following:

- Is there a study guide for the course that will help me to understand the content? Perhaps your instructor has developed or could recommend one.
- Does the institution offer tutoring, on-site and/or virtual, for the content area? Perhaps the instructor has designed ways to provide learning assistance support to students.
- Are there computer software programs available that I could purchase to help me with the content?

Third, if you have a disability that requires accommodation, explore the services and accommodations that are available to you through the host institution. You will want to know about the specific technical and learning support available to help ensure your access to and success in distance learning courses. You also will want to be clear about your rights and responsibilities as well as the responsibilities of the host institution in accommodating your disability. Here are a few questions that will help guide you:

- Is there a specific department and/or individual with whom I need to be in contact? In essence, what is the procedure for identifying myself and my disability to the institution? It is important for you to know that you are not required to disclose that you have a disability to a postsecondary institution *unless* you are seeking an accommodation.
- What services does the host institution have to accommodate students with disabilities? Who is eligible to receive services?
- What specific services are provided to support my disability?
- What documentation is required? Does the institution have any provision for diagnostic testing? If so, how do I gain access to such a service?

- Once an individual is identified, who is responsible for making the arrangements for accommodations (e.g., identifying a note taker, providing information in an alternative format)?
- To what extent does the institution work closely with outside agencies in providing accommodations?
- Who is notified of my disability? How are they notified? Who keeps the records of my needs? Who has access to these records?
- What support systems exist for students with disabilities (e.g., student groups), and how can distance learners participate in them?

Although a good start, having the answers to these questions may not be enough. As a distance learner with disabilities, you will need some very specific answers to questions regarding technical and learning support. For example, if you have a hearing, visual, and/or physical disability, you should ask questions such as these:

- What formats are available to accommodate students with hearing, visual, and/or physical disabilities? In general, what support is available for each format?
- How is interpreter support provided? Is it available at the local receive site or through video relay interpreters (VRIs)? If the support is through VRIs, what services are available locally to support my access to class interaction?
- Whom should I contact if I experience technical difficulties during the broadcasting of a telecourse? How should I contact that person, and what response should I expect? For example, if I am deaf and the course I am taking is to be captioned, what action do I take if there is a malfunction? What accommodations will be made for me to get the material I missed if the malfunction continues?
- What about similar support for computer-based courses? What office or individual is responsible for providing technical support? What hours will the office or individual be available? My needs might well range from hardware compatibility to problems with accompanying sound. What kind of support should I expect in recognizing these needs?
- What about access to distance learning sites and facilities for people with physical disabilities? A receive site on the third floor of a classroom building that has no elevator access would pose significant difficulties for those with mobility problems.

If you have a documented *learning disability*, you should consider questions that relate to assignments, assessments, and other types of assistance. A few such questions are as follows:

- Is the syllabus clear regarding the assignments/that are required? What accommodations will be made if I am qualified to receive additional time to complete assignments or need to complete them in a different format, such as verbal versus written?
- As with assignments, what methods will be used to assess students? Are there accommodations for students whose disability requires a need for additional time for exams?
- What assistance is available, either through the instructor or through the institutional provider, for additional help?

Additional information and resources regarding accommodations for postsecondary students with disabilities are available on the Guide's website.

Fourth, be an informed advocate for yourself! As with other aspects of distance learning, you need to be an informed advocate for yourself and your needs. This is good general advice for all distance learning students and particularly important for distance learning students with disabilities. If you are a distance learning student with a disability, be sure that you have a good understanding of your particular disability so that you are able to articulate your strengths, limitations, as well as the compensating techniques and accommodations that work best for you. Be informed about your rights and responsibilities and the responsibilities of the host institution. The U. S. Department of Education has put together a pamphlet entitled *Students with Disabilities Preparing for Postsecondary Education: Know Your Rights and Responsibilities* specifically for this purpose. It is available online at **www.ed.gov/ocr**. Also remember that it is your responsibility as a student to report your needs for accommodation to the institution and to supply any required documentation. It is then the responsibility of the institution to provide those accommodations that are determined reasonable.

To summarize, participating in distance learning does not mean you are totally on your own. There are ways to connect with faculty members and other students to develop small learning communities for mutual support and learning. In the event you need academic assistance and/or accommodation for a disability, there are avenues you can pursue to get the help you need. Here are some questions you can ask yourself, faculty members, and institutions as you explore your own needs for connection and support and how to meet those needs:

- What are my preferences regarding contact with faculty members and other students? Am I more of an independent learner than not? If not, does the course I am taking or contemplating provide the opportunities, virtual and otherwise, for interaction with others that I need?

- What kinds of learning assistance are available to distance learning students? Are campus-based services open to those in distance learning? What provisions have been made to support those who might be having difficulty with content who do not live within commuting distance to the host institution?

- What is the process for disclosing a disability and pursuing accommodation for that disability? What type and level of accommodation should I expect?

Expecting Support and Assistance Is Okay

What's important to remember is that although you may not be on campus you are a student taking a course or courses from an institution. It is perfectly acceptable to express your needs for communication with faculty members and other students, as well as needs regarding learning assistance. It also is perfectly reasonable to expect that if resources are made available to other students served by the institution, they should also be available in some form to you as a distance learner. You should evaluate your needs and determine what the institution provides to meet them. Be aware that not all institutions will be able to provide the services you may want or need. They should be clear about what they do provide in materials given to students. If institutions aren't clear, or what you need to be successful is not provided by the institution or faculty members teaching the courses, then you should pursue other distance learning alternatives. Distance learning is here to stay and many opportunities will continue to emerge for students who either prefer or require this educational option.

HEALTH AND WELLNESS: THERE IS A RELATIONSHIP TO COLLEGE SUCCESS

Setting goals, prioritizing roles, and ensuring that you have the academic and social support you need are important to succeeding in distance learning. However, at the end of the day, if you haven't paid enough attention to issues of personal health and wellness, you risk not completing your courses because of illness. *Each of us has developed an approach to health that is personal. The primary recommendation here is that you evaluate your approach and make adjustments as you see fit to help ensure that you remain healthy.*

This is not a handbook about eating well and taking care of yourself. But because it is a guide to helping you succeed in learning, topics of health and wellness are essential. *There is a relationship between being healthy and effective learning.* For example, it is clear that the things you do to take care of your body—eating well, exercising regularly, and getting sufficient rest—all have positive effects on your ability to concentrate and on your memory. Being healthy also affects your ability to effectively handle stress (see Chapter 6 for more information about stress management). Do we all take good care of our health? Probably not, but we should. Let's examine the issues related to diet, exercise, and rest.

Worksheet #4, "Health & Wellness: A Short Self-Assessment and Plan for Change," was developed to help guide you through the self-assessment questions asked in the next section. The worksheet is available on the Guide's website.

The Basics of Good Health: Diet, Exercise, and Rest

Diet.　Most of us already know about good nutrition, but we need to be reminded of it before we reach for that "study snack," which usually consists of a bag of chips, a bowl of popcorn, a soda, and perhaps even a bunch of chocolate chip cookies. By themselves, and in moderation, these snacks are not necessarily going to be detrimental to your health and well-being. However, when they are coupled with the absence of a healthy breakfast and the grabbing of a "quick lunch" at the local burger palace—to be eaten while driving to your next meeting or class—they can pose a problem. So, we really ought to explore healthier ways of eating.

In brief, guidelines suggest that you should

- eat a variety of foods.
- maintain a healthy weight.

- choose a diet low in fat, saturated fat, and cholesterol.
- choose a diet with plenty of vegetables, fruits, and grains.
- use sugars only in moderation.
- use salt and sodium only in moderation.
- drink alcoholic beverages only in moderation.

Much has been written about developing good eating habits. There are additional resources on our website to explore if you wish. For our purposes, it is more important that you determine how closely you want to follow these guidelines and make adjustments accordingly. Do a self-assessment by asking yourself questions such as the following. Use the spaces provided or Worksheet #4 on the website to record your answers:

- Where is your diet relative to these guidelines?

_____

- How satisfied are you with your current diet?

_____

- What changes are you ready to make (if any) to come closer to your ideal level of satisfaction?

_____

Exercise. An effective exercise program does not have to involve lots of expensive equipment and a lot of time. Participating in some type of aerobic exercise effectively improves your body functioning and thus your ability to concentrate and perform tasks more efficiently. There are many books and references, including videotapes, to help you develop an aerobic exercise plan that works for you. Be sure to check with your physician to help you design a plan that *works* for you—not one that may be detrimental to your health.

As with diet, take the time to do a self-assessment. Here are some

questions to ask yourself. Use the spaces provided or Worksheet #4 on the website to record your answers:

- Do I have an exercise plan?

_____

- Am I satisfied with how I feel and my general sense of health?

_____

- What changes can I make to bring myself closer to what I believe to be my optimum level of health?

_____

Rest.   In the section on setting your role priorities, you were asked how much sleep you require to be at your best performance. You were also asked when you were most alert and prepared to learn (morning, afternoon, evening). These questions assume that you require some level of rest to ensure that you are operating at your maximum effectiveness. The body needs time to rejuvenate itself and to relax and recuperate from the day's events and activities. However, it is common knowledge that each of us requires a different amount of sleep and rest. You need to pay attention to your body's need for rest and ensure that you meet this need by building it into your priorities and daily time management plan. If you don't, you will find that you are doing justice neither to your health nor to your classes.

Following are more questions for self-assessment. Use the spaces provided or Worksheet #4 on the website to record your answers:

- How much rest do you require?

_____

- Are you getting it? Why or why not?

_____

- If you aren't getting enough rest, is it affecting your performance at work, at school, or with your family?

_____

- If so, how can you make changes to accommodate your need for additional rest?

_____

Where Does Fun Fit into All This?

Recall the story about Cheryl, the wife, mother, and professional woman who decided to pursue college courses. For her, leisure time was not something she was willing to compromise. The small amount of time she allocated to leisure activities was essential for her to maintain a healthy outlook on life.

What is leisure for one is not leisure for another. Leisure is often defined as recreation. Some use a more literal translation of recreation and talk about leisure as a way to re-create oneself. In this regard, leisure is defined in its broadest context and would include areas related to the psychological, physical, and intellectual self. In this context, some may view taking college courses as an activity they pursue for fun. Others may find course work stressful and look to other activities for their enjoyment. *What is your definition of leisure?* Use Worksheet #4 on the website to record your answers. However you define leisure, it is important to identify at least some time during the week for activities related to "having fun."

Handbooks developed to improve student success often include sections on health and being healthy. Issues related to health are included because they are important and there is a relationship between health and doing your best academically. If you are tired, your concentration is affected and, consequently, so is your ability to recall and retain information. The same is true if you are ill. Although you may intuitively know that maintaining your health is important to doing well in your courses, you may not take the necessary steps to ensure that you remain healthy. For example, in an already hectic life with many role commitments and responsibilities, it is often personal time—rest and leisure—that suffers. Remember the story about Sharon, the married professional woman with two children in college? Her experience in juggling her commitments and academic workload is how many of us manage to "get everything done": we burn the proverbial candle at both ends, hoping the struggle will be short-lived.

A personal decision to change behaviors should be based on an evaluation of your current behaviors related to your health. What are your current practices, and how do these relate to where you want to be? If there is a mismatch, you can make the changes necessary to achieve the desired level of health. The following questions can help you begin to make an initial assessment of your personal approach to health and wellness:

- **Diet:** Do you generally follow the guidelines noted in the diet section of this chapter?

- **Exercise:** Do you exercise regularly?
- **Rest:** Do you know how much rest you need to be at your best and do you ensure that you get it?
- **Fun:** What do you define as leisure and how does it relate to your priorities?

For each of these areas, determine your level of satisfaction with your current behavior and then decide where you would like to be with each of these areas. Is there a mismatch? If so, you need to develop a plan for change. The resources on the Guide's website can help you learn more about each of the discussed areas and develop strategies to help you achieve your desired goals for your health and wellness.

SUMMARY: A FINAL NOTE

This chapter has identified those areas related to self that can serve as barriers to success in distance learning. Among the most important of these are unclear goals; interference of other commitments; lack of a system of academic and social support; and, finally, lack of attention to issues of health and wellness. All of these areas are personal and depend on one's own individual desires, needs, and priorities. At the end of each section, questions were listed as tools to help you make decisions about your priorities, your learning needs, and your personal health and wellness. The fundamental questions of this chapter include the following:

- What are your reasons for being a student?
- What are your role priorities and how does being a student fit within them?
- What kind of support do you need to be a successful student?
- What resources are available to you through your instructor, other students, or the host institution to meet your support needs?
- What is your assessment of your own health and wellness? If there is a mismatch between your reality and your ideal, how can you design a plan that will move you closer to your ideal?

If you understand your goals, set your priorities, identify your learning needs, and actively seek to meet them, and take care of your health, you will be well on your way to addressing those personal issues that can become barriers to your success in distance learning.

www.DLGuide.info

Visit this website for additional information and activities.

CHAPTER 6

BECOMING A BETTER DISTANCE LEARNING STUDENT

Steps to Success

In this chapter you will

- ◆ find specific detailed guidance to help you succeed in your course of studies

- ◆ gain a new understanding of learning and studying

- ◆ learn that succeeding as a student means really learning how to learn and enjoying the learning

- ◆ learn how to make steady progress toward achieving your goal of a degree or certificate

- ◆ learn effective methods of studying, note taking, time management, stress management, reading, writing, and test taking

- ◆ learn how to improve your computer and Internet literacy and where to access online learning resources for greater success in your classes as well as for lifelong learning

It is critically important that you learn to improve your distance learning performance because, as a distance learner, you are more on your own than most classroom learners—consequently, you must take more responsibility for your own learning.

The chapter begins with general ideas about learning and then teaches specific techniques. If you are eager to look at the techniques before reading about the background ideas, jump right into the section "Study Guides." But it's important that you also read the "Learning to Learn" section because you need to know how and why specific techniques work if you are to modify them to best fit your own circumstances and learning style.

INTRODUCTION

Students who are new to distance learning are often concerned about how well they will be able to perform in their courses, and whether distance learning courses will be harder than traditional classroom courses. You've already learned, in Chapter 1, that there are many varieties and mixes of distance education that use different modalities. The first thing to recognize about this sprawling variety of distance learning courses is that you will find some delivery modes more appealing than others.

Try to find the mode of instruction that works best for you. Some people do well and prefer studying on their own, whereas others need the stimulation of interaction (introverts versus extroverts). Some people do best hearing material presented, whereas others do best seeing material in books and videos (visual and auditory learners). Still others need to interact with the materials by drawing or moving objects (kinesthetic learners). Different learning styles match well or poorly with different modes of instruction; try to learn about what works and doesn't work for you.

Whatever delivery medium is used in a course, you should take advantage of every opportunity to use all the available learning resources. Use whatever way you can to make contact with your instructor, your advisor, your fellow students, and learning support staff. The first basic guideline for becoming a more effective learner is this: Communicate early and often with whomever can be of help. Don't wait until you are doing poorly in a class before seeking help. By making contact early and letting people know who you are, you establish a learner–teacher relationship that will be available when you really need it.

> ### TIP | Online Resources
>
> References for this chapter are available on the companion website. You will also find links to numerous additional how-to-study resources that are available online.

Distance learning courses are generally just as effective as traditional classroom courses, no matter what modality is used for instruction. If given a choice, most students would prefer to take classes that involve direct contacts with the instructor and other students. Students usually choose distance education courses because of the convenience and flexibility of taking a class that does not require that they be at a certain place at a certain time. Distance learning students are generally more motivated to succeed in their studies and to learn effective techniques of learning and studying. So let's get started.

LEARNING TO LEARN

The phrase *learning to learn* appears frequently in how-to-study books, but this section is concerned with attitudes and ideas about learning, rather than specific study techniques. It will be worthwhile to examine a few core facts and ideas about learning before getting into details about improving your studying. We'll be building on the learning skills that you already have. The object is to become more aware of what enters into the act of learning so that you can learn even more efficiently and effectively—and become more confident about what you are doing.

Learning more about how you learn is something like reading your computer manual. You can certainly use the computer without ever reading the user's manual, but you'll be better prepared to care for the computer, handle emergencies, and use applications more effectively and efficiently if you read the manual.

The second basic guideline for becoming a more effective learner is this: Always remember that all learning is to some extent self-learning and must be self-guided and self-motivated. The more you know about yourself as a learner, the better you will be at guiding your own learning. Even if you have the best teacher in the world sitting at your elbow in a tutorial setting, you will not learn, remember, and use what you learn if you do not put forth a conscious, well-informed effort.

Here are six interesting facts and ideas from the fields of psychology and education to orient your study of learning techniques.

Interesting Fact #1: Effective Learning Requires Active Organizing

Some of the best insights about how to learn come from reading what has been written about helping teachers teach. Teachers are taught to organize course material into segments that can be ordered and assimilated. Unfortunately, the act of organizing for meaning is something that students often disregard and are not taught to do. Instead, students stay passive about their learning, while teachers do the active learning. Animal experiments have demonstrated that rats that are barged through a water maze will not learn the route of the maze, whereas rats that swim the maze do learn the route. We've all experienced the difference between being driven to a place and not learning how to get there versus driving to a destination and learning the route.

Of course, students will use the organization already provided by the instructor and by their textbooks, but students *must* make the effort to be in the driver's seat and not be merely a passenger on a route chosen by the teacher. Being in the driver's seat means to actively think, question, and consider alternative ways of doing or saying things. In other words, you must intend and plan to learn.

Interesting Fact #2: It Does Take Time to Assimilate New Learning

The three key processes in memory are typically described as encoding, storage, and retrieval. Encoding involves getting information into memory. Storage involves maintaining encoded information in memory over time. Retrieval involves recovering information from memory stores. The level of processing of information is closely related to how effectively it will be stored and retrieved. Shallow processing encodes nothing more than the physical structure or a stimulus: Is a word written in CAPITAL letters? Intermediate processing emphasizes the sound of a word: Does a word rhyme with "bee"? Deep processing emphasizes the meaning of a word: Would the word fit in the

---

What About Cramming?

Should you ever "cram" for your studies? Well, the "should" hardly matters because you undoubtedly will be in a position at some point when you just haven't had enough time to study adequately and will need to cram as much learning as possible into a very short time. Spaced learning over time has been shown to be the most effective for promoting deeper encoding, longer storage, and better retrieval. There is no denying, however, that cramming can work when the material being learned does not need to be retained for a long time. Although you may need to cram occasionally, try to avoid doing it as a regular practice if you want to optimize your long-term learning. Recent research has shown that, at the biochemical level, the production of new proteins in the brain is required for memories to become permanent. Such production takes time.

---

sentence "He met a _____ on the street"? Studying will be most effective when it involves deep processing for meaning rather than shallower processing.

Interesting Fact #3: Feelings Are Important in Remembering

If you doubt that feelings are important for remembering, just think about the last time you had a strong emotional experience, such as a near miss in an automobile collision, a sporting accident, or an angry encounter. We usually can vividly remember such incidents, recalling exactly what happened just before, during, and after the emotional event. Indeed, sometimes the problem is how to stop remembering traumatic events; such memories interfere with our everyday lives if they become intrusive.

A less dramatic but more pervasive illustration of the role of emotion in memory is found in the familiar "tip-of-the-tongue" phenomenon. This happens when we are sure that we know the answer to some question, such as the name of a person or place, but can't recall (retrieve) what we are sure that we know. Most people experience this phenomenon about once a week, and the frequency with which it occurs does increase with age. Numerous research studies have shown that when we feel that we know something, the odds are that we do indeed know the fact or place name or person's name that we can't immediately produce. Given more time or hints, or if asked to choose the correct answer from among a number of similar but wrong answers, we are very likely to come up with the correct answer. Feelings can be an accurate guide to what we know and don't know and to what we can and can't remember.

One reason why students should always try to be active in their learning rather than passive is that active learning provides more feeling cues than passive learning. It is sometimes difficult to get excited about material that we must learn when we don't find the material intrinsically interesting. You will generate just the right level of feeling compatible with learning if you try to answer questions when studying or note taking, rather than merely reading or listening. A helpful tension will be created when you pose a question for which you do not yet have the answer.

Interesting Fact #4: Adults Approach Learning Differently Than Children

The age-old belief that adults are more limited than children in the ability to learn new things is false. The "old dogs can't learn new tricks theory" was disproved early in the history of experimental psychology. In 1928, pioneering educational psychologist Edward Thorndike wrote, "Adults can learn rather easily and rapidly, and probably could learn much more than they do." He went on to say, "Adults learn much less than they might partly because they underestimate their power of learning, and partly because of unpleasant attention and comment . . . [and] adults learn less than they might because they do not care enough about learning."* Thus, if you are apprehensive about your ability to succeed in adult distance education courses, remember: You can do it!

Although adults are able to learn most things as quickly and effectively as children, there are differences in the ways that children and adults approach learning. The basic notion is that adults are more self-guided in their learning than children. Because of their wider experience, adults can bring more to the learning task than children can, and adults can take away more to apply to their everyday lives.

---

*Thorndike, E., Bregman, E., Tilton, J. W., and Woodyard, E. *Adult Learning*. New York: Macmillan, 1928.

It is essential that adult learning be learner centered, because adults will not do many tasks just because "the teacher said to do it." For adults, learning needs to make sense. Consequently, if you do not find the material in your course inherently interesting, you will need to work to add value and interest to the subject for yourself.

Interesting Fact #5: There Are Different Ways of Being Smart

For many years, the theory of "general intelligence" dominated the fields of psychology and education. You took an intelligence test and got one score that labeled you as smart or dumb or normal. For the last three decades, psychologists have been more disposed to think of "multiple intelligences" and to believe that there are different dimensions of being intelligent. Harvard psychologist Howard Gardner has identified eight distinct intelligences:

1. **Visual–spatial** learners think in terms of physical space. They are comfortable with models, graphics, charts, and drawings.
2. **Bodily–kinesthetic** learners have a keen sense of body awareness and learn well through physical activity and role-playing.
3. **Musical** learners are sensitive to rhythm and sound. They may study better with music in the background.
4. **Intrapersonal** learners understand themselves well but may shy away from others. They can be taught through independent study and introspection.
5. **Interpersonal** learners relate well to others, noticing moods, motivations, and feelings. They can learn through cooperative learning and teamwork.
6. **Linguistic** learners use words effectively. They like reading, playing word games, or making up poetry or stories.
7. **Logical–mathematical** learners think conceptually, abstractly, and are able to see and explore patterns and relationships.
8. **Naturalistic** learners understand their environment. They are interested in ecological balance and may study better in natural surroundings.

These different intelligences, strengths, or competencies may each have its own developmental history. In other words, it would be possible for a person to be very advanced in one competency at an early age (say musical intelligence) but not attain much competency in another intelligence (say interpersonal intelligence) until a much later age. A valuable insight for adults is that lifelong learning can be thought of not just as the continuing effort to learn new content and skills but as the lifelong development of each person's multiple intelligences. We aren't stuck with just being "not musical," "not mathematical," "not word minded," "not artistic," or "not athletic." We can recognize that some of our competencies emerge much earlier or much later than others do.

The multiple intelligences approach can be applied directly to the educational setting. You can recognize that any course or subject matter will engage different intelligences, and that you bring more development to one subject than to others. Some subjects will require that you give yourself basic help, whereas other subjects will be easy because they call upon competencies that you've already developed.

Interesting Fact #6: Some Schools Fit Some Students Better Than Others

Extensive education research has shown that how well students do in school depends on the school–student fit. Students who do mediocre work in one college may do very well in another, not because one college is easier than the other, but because there is a better fit of student to college in the second institution. This fit helps the student to become involved with the institution, rather than staying uninvolved. Keep this fact in mind when you explore distance learning institutions. You need to find a college that fits you, rather than try to fit yourself into the mold of the college. You need to become involved in working with the faculty, the staff, your advisors, and other students at the college that you choose. To repeat some earlier advice, you may wish to take a class or two to see if you are comfortable with distance education and the style of the instructors and advisors at the college.

If you are like most distance learning students, you will be reentering higher education rather than starting college for the first time. Adult students are often self-conscious about their status as reentry students and frequently feel inferior to students who persisted in their degree efforts without dropping out. However, statistics show that of every 100 entrants to higher education, only about 45 eventually will obtain a bachelor's degree (another 13 to 14 will earn an associate's degree). These statistics mean that students who succeed are in the *minority*. The majority, 55 percent, drop out and stay out. By returning to college as an adult, you are taking the first step in putting yourself among the minority of students who eventually will succeed. "Stopping out" for a time is different from dropping out and staying out. Among students who leave college, nearly 30 percent do reenroll.

Other research has shown that it is the quality of the student's effort that predicts success in college rather than fixed factors such as parental education, race, age, and gender. When a student commits to doing well and puts forth a quality effort, then that student is likely to succeed. Various theories have been propounded about how college helps students to change. They all focus on the college–student fit, which will facilitate student involvement with her or his own education and with the educators at the institution.

STUDY GUIDES

Now that you have an overview about learning to learn, let's get into the particulars of how-to-study techniques. Every student who enters or reenters college would benefit from spending some time reading about study techniques. Those who are already good students will learn a few new tricks. Those who aren't can learn the mechanics that contribute to being an effective learner.

This chapter is intended to provide a general orientation to becoming a better distance learner and specific recommendations about techniques to apply. You will find more than enough suggestions to get you started in your new study efforts. There are numerous other study guides to help you discover the ideas and techniques that work best for you. There also are a number of study aids available online, many of which can be found at the Guide's website.

Most guidebooks include coverage not just of study techniques but also of time management, reading, note taking, writing papers, taking tests, and all the other activities that enter into being an effective student. However, few guidebooks are directed specifically at adult students who are taking courses and attempting to complete their degrees via distance learning (like this Guide). Therefore, it will be necessary for you to adapt some of these study recommendations into steps that you can apply in distance learning courses. Whichever study guide you read, be sure to apply the techniques promptly to your course. It does no good to just read about studying more effectively—you must put the techniques to work.

The SQ4R Study Method

The reliable, much-used SQ4R method has been described in innumerable study guides. SQ4R means, "Scan (or survey), Question, Read, Recite (or Rite), Recall, and Review." As a technique, it manages to capture much (but not everything) about being an active learner rather than a passive learner.

Imagine that you are in a typical course with typical expectations. Your assignment is to read the first two chapters of the assigned textbook in week one of the course and be prepared to take a quiz the following week. Here's how you would apply the SQ4R method:

- **Scan or Survey.**   Don't begin by reading the first assigned chapter. Instead scan or survey it. By surveying a chapter, you get an overview and you gain some familiarity with the main terms and phrases. You are reading to see *how* the chapter is organized rather than trying to understand *what* is said. Don't read word by word, just scan. If the author provides an outline or a summary, do read that more carefully.

- **Question.**   Go back over the chapter and formulate questions based on the parts or sections that you've identified as important. The author may have provided questions at the end of the chapter for you, but it is essential that you *make up your own questions based on how you first see the chapter*. You will be revising your questions (and your answers) as you read the chapter more carefully, so don't worry about developing precise, complete questions on the first pass.

- **Read.**   Now that you've formulated your questions, you are ready to read the chapter carefully and purposefully, and to answer the questions that you identified. As you read, you may find that you want to reword some of your questions and perhaps add questions that you had overlooked in your first survey. (We'll explore the types of reading in the section "Reading Guides.") The key to effective reading is to read for understanding. The self-guided test of your understanding is whether you can answer your own questions.

- **Recite or Rite.**   The key in this step is to use your own words to answer your questions based on the reading that you just did. You *must* answer in your own words rather than merely repeating what you read, but be careful that you don't inadvertently change the meaning of the question or the author's points. Don't write too much, just enough to sketch your answers. Pretend that you're taking an exam and answer in the way that you know will be required in the course. If you will be writing short essay exams, make your answers that length; if you will be taking multiple choice tests, make your answers shorter.

- **Recall.** When you recall, you are practicing to remember. Go back through the questions and without looking at your notes or written answers come up with the answers again. Leave a little time between the recite step and the recall step, so that you can truly see if you remember enough to reproduce the answer.

- **Review.** Reviewing depends on timing. In this example, you would go on to read and apply the SQ4R method to the second chapter before undertaking your review. You must decide when to review your questions and again recall your answers, depending on the exam schedule for the course. If you will be tested on the assigned materials weekly, you must review weekly; if you will only be taking a midterm and a final, you need to review in several staggered sessions before those exams. Do not try to apply the entire SQ4R method just before an exam. Reviewing is dependent on completion of the previous steps; you can't review what you haven't given yourself time to study.

Exercise 6.1

Take 15 minutes to apply this simple study method to this chapter by doing the first two steps. You've already read to this point, but start over again by scanning the entire chapter, and then make up some questions based on what you see as the most important ideas of the chapter. Come back to this point when you are done surveying and formulating questions. You'll have a much different perspective on what is being said than you would if you had simply read straight through and done nothing else.

Concept (or Mental) Mapping

To learn effectively, you must take control of your own learning. The way to do that is to become a teacher to yourself; for yourself; and, if necessary, by yourself. By thinking like a teacher when you approach a learning task, you will be putting yourself in the most advantageous position for learning. Your full role as a learner is to be a teacher—your own teacher, for your own learning.

Every adult who is reading these words already is a successful learner at a number of things. Although you may not have been very successful at academic learning previously, think about something that you do well. Perhaps it is a sport, cooking, music, something artistic, or something at your work. Undoubtedly, this activity required a learning period that lasted for years, during which you acquired a set of skills. You also gained a mental map of how to do what you do. Now, you must learn to form a mental map, or concept map, for every academic course that you take.

All of us construct and use mental maps each day. The most common experience of mental mapping is when we travel to a different section of a city. At first, everything looks unfamiliar; we have no detailed mental map at all. Our first "map" is like the old maps of the New World in the days of Columbus, where everything beyond a certain border was labeled "Unknown." Pointing to the unknown *is* a kind of map, because at least we know where the unknown begins. As we traverse an area, certain landmarks emerge, and our mental map becomes more elaborate, perhaps by adding a street name, a church spire, or a gas station. If we travel the route often, the mental map becomes very elaborate, so that we can actually anticipate what we will see along the route. Interestingly, even elaborate mental maps are likely to have gaps, just because we don't learn what is around every corner in every direction. We learn only what we need to reach our destinations. Another interesting fact is that different people have very different mental maps, although they are all able to reach a given destination. This is because the features that are important in one person's map are not important in another person's.

Sports provide an instructive example concerning mental maps. A number of research studies have demonstrated that it is *more* effective to divide practice time for a sport into mental practice *and* physical practice than to spend all the time in one or the other. It is just as important to visualize the sequence of movements involved in performing a basketball free throw and to imagine the sequence of sensations and positions to be executed as it is to actually practice free throws. Without a clear mental picture of what to do, an aspiring athlete will introduce variations in the movement, making it difficult to repeat the pattern reliably.

The point of this discussion about mental, or concept, maps is *that a fundamental part of learning must be focused on the construction of a mental map for any subject that is being studied and for all the parts of the subject*. Without developing a concept map that becomes increasingly detailed and interconnected, students are simply memorizing. Even memorizing is almost impossible without constructing some learning plan. It is possible to apply the SQ4R method as a drill and to overlook the need to couple it with concept mapping. Only when a study method is coupled with a conscious effort to form concept maps does learning become powerful and efficient.

Of course, the map is not the actual place. Maps are abstract representations of places. Similarly, the map of a subject or course is not the course. If you memorize the map, you will not have learned the course; but the map does help guide your learning in the course. Using someone else's map can be helpful, but what is *most* valuable in learning is constructing your own map. With your map, you are traveling through the subject as a newcomer and not an expert. The expert's map will be too detailed and too layered for the beginner. (See the companion website for references about concept maps and for software to facilitate mapping.)

The value of doodling. The easiest way to get started with concept mapping in your studies is to indulge in the common art of doodling. As soon as you approach a course, a book, or an assignment, be sure to have plenty of doodle paper at hand so that you can simply draw connections among words, ideas, and methods as you read. Don't try to be artistic or produce engineering diagrams—just doodle. You will throw away most of your doodles, but you may end up with a few that so clearly map what you've been reading or hearing in a lecture that you will want to keep them to guide you in further studies and pre-exam reviews.

The kind of doodling described here is very different from the doodling that you might do when you pay *no* attention to what you are reading or hearing. Study doodling helps you to organize and identify important points. Drawing cartoons or sketch doodling is just a way to avoid boredom.

Exercise 6.2

Try doodling right now. Take a sheet of paper and draw some lines, arrows, boxes, triangles, circles, question marks, exclamation points, and other figures that connect the different words and ideas that you've been reading in this section on study guides; print the **WORDS** and **IDEAS** in big, bold print. Remember that the purpose of your doodles is to represent the mental map that you are developing. It is fine if there are places where the doodles show that you don't know what connects with what or what leads to what—by knowing that you don't know, you'll be preparing yourself to learn more. Doodles are visual statements and visual question marks. Study doodling provides an easy, preliminary way to organize and map what you are trying to learn.

The "I CARE" system.   Professors Bob Hoffman and Donn Ritchie of San Diego State University have been working with instructors in the California State University system to help them create online courses. The core idea is that both students and instructors benefit by having a mental model of their course. Each module of their online workshop is organized around what they call the "I CARE" five-step system—Introduction, Connect, Apply, Reflect, and Extend:

- The *introduction* places the module in the context of the course as a whole.

- The *connect* section presents new information in context by using charts, diagrams, illustrations, or other tools to map the new information to the other parts of the course, that is, what came before in other modules and what will follow.

- *Apply* is the practice section of the module, which is whatever can be done to utilize the information and concepts in the module.

- The *reflect* section asks students to reflect on what they've just learned—from responding to questions from the instructor to journal entries to peer exchanges or other reflective activities.

- Finally, *extend* is where more is added to what was done in that module. It uses everything from evaluating what was presented and how meaningful/useful/interesting it was to providing additional resources.

Distance learning students may apply the I CARE system to their own learning. The way to do that is to take the books, assignments, syllabi, lecture notes, tapes, software, and other resources available to you for a course and attempt to actively organize those materials in the same way that you would if you were an instructor. The difference between the way you would undertake this activity and the way an instructor would is that you would apply the I CARE system after you looked at the organization and materials. Your instructor will have drawn on years of experience to organize the course, which allows you to draw on the instructor's organization as you do your own.

As you can see, this is a much more sophisticated and demanding activity than simply applying the SQ4R method to assignments, but the two activities do overlap. Think of the SQ4R method as the micromethod to use when studying a specific assignment and the I CARE system as the macromethod to apply to the course as a whole. By using both, you will be working on the details that must be mastered for succeeding in a course and the big picture and framework that you must construct if you are to be successful at long-term learning.

Concept mapping is a way to think about what you are doing when you apply the I CARE system. Doodling is an activity that can be applied on the way to developing more elaborate concept maps. If you are reading a textbook that is well organized and listening to lectures that are interestingly presented and well linked to the text and the syllabus, then you've already been given a major framework, which you can simply improve for yourself by using the I CARE method. If the materials are more scattered, then you will need to do more work to organize them. To be an effective learner, you must make the effort to develop your own concept maps. Without that effort, you will never be in control of your own learning.

NOTE TAKING

The most important thing to remember when taking notes is this: Do not write down every word. Think of what you are doing as "note making" rather than "note taking." When you make notes, you are trying to record the main points—you are not taking dictation. Distance learning students who listen to or view audio- or videotaped lectures (or lectures on CDs or DVDs) or listen to or view audio- or videostreams from Web-based courses actually have an advantage over students who listen to lectures in a classroom—they can rewind to review a section of the lecture that wasn't clear. The disadvantage for distance students is that they can't ask questions during or just after the lecture. To overcome this disadvantage and to avoid listening passively, make believe you are listening to the lecture live and pretend you can ask any question at any time. Always write your questions among your notes, and take the first opportunity to look for answers in the text or handouts. If you can't find answers that clarify the lectures from your print resources, then be sure to communicate with the instructor by whatever means you have (e.g., email, fax, telephone).

Five-Stage Note Taking

A popular technique for taking notes is the five-stage Cornell System, developed by Walter Pauk. The five stages are Record, Reduce, Recite,

Reflect, and Review (you will notice some overlap with the SQ4R study method):

- **Record.** Draw a vertical line from the top to the bottom of a page (use enough pages to cover the lecture). The left column will be your recall column. Leave it blank until after the lecture. During the lecture, your emphasis is on active listening. In the right column, record and sketch as much information as you believe is needed and important while listening to the lecture. Use an outline or a doodle map. Write down exactly what the instructor is saying only if he or she indicates that it is important to get a sentence or phrase precisely. Always do the prereading that is recommended before the lecture so you will know what not to include in your notes because you already have notes from your SQ4R studying. Write your notes in "telegraphese" rather than complete sentences, and do use sentence phrases and word outlines that would not be acceptable for a formal essay. Remember that you are the only one who needs to understand your notes.

- **Reduce.** As soon after the lecture as you can, condense your notes into a few words, abbreviations, or phrases in the recall column on the left. In effect you are preparing "prompt cards" that will jog your memory of the original lecture.

- **Recite.** Cover your notes and try to say what is in them in your own words. In doing so, you are giving a minilecture or summary of the original lecture. If you need prompts, look at the words or phrases on your "prompt cards." After you go through the recitation, uncover your notes and check yourself for completeness and accuracy.

- **Reflect.** Allow a few days to pass before doing this stage. Then, reread your notes and think about how they relate to your reading and to lectures that preceded or followed this one. You may want to modify or correct your notes based on your expanded understanding.

- **Review.** Do *spaced* reviews of all your accumulated notes over the weeks of the term; as you do this reviewing, continue to annotate and modify your original notes so that they become both more elaborated and more organized.

Although doodling is not a part of the Cornell System, you can use additional pages to add conceptual mapping doodles to your lecture notes, especially in the reflect and review stages.

TIME AND STRESS MANAGEMENT

There are no time management secrets that will allow you to convert 24 hours in a day into 48 hours. So, the first thing to do in managing your time is to *realistically* evaluate how much time you have for studying. The general rule is to allow two to three hours of outside study time per week for each credit hour of a course. For a five-credit course you should study 10 to 15 hours a week, in addition to whatever time you put in on distance learning. *Don't sign up for more hours of course work than you can handle.* Adult students who are working full-time and involved in family and community responsibilities should not try to carry the same number of credit hours as an 18- to 25-year-old on-campus student who is not working. It's impossible!

Many students returning to college are advised to take no more than one or two classes in their first term. In this way, they can succeed at their first courses, as well as learn how much time they have available and how much they need for studying (see Chapter 5 for a discussion of balancing study and other responsibilities). This advice may prompt you to say, "But I'll never finish. I'll never get my degree." Not true! You will be able to finish, and you will be able to add more courses per term once you devise a study schedule and develop a study routine. A sure way to never complete your degree is to fail your first courses. Start a pattern of success and you will continue to succeed as a student. Start a pattern of failure and you will likely drop out.

Most traditional students study far too little and are then puzzled when they fail or do poorly in classes, and they become dismayed when

they drop out. Results from a recent UCLA Higher Education Research Institute's annual survey of college first-year students showed that 66 percent spent less than six hours per week studying (this includes reading, reviewing notes, writing papers, and doing research). Traditional students sometimes view adult students as "grade busters" because they score well above the class average. Adults who are returning to school usually do well because they realize they must put in adequate study time. If you manage your time so that you study two to three hours weekly outside class for every credit hour that you take and do not sign up for too many credit hours, you undoubtedly will do better in your courses than students who do not acknowledge that studying takes time.

The Lakein ABC Method of Time Management

The essence of the time management method developed by Allan Lakein is to list, prioritize, and check. First, list the jobs or tasks that you know you need to do during the coming week. The order of the list makes no difference—simply make the list. You can add to the list during the week if other things come up or if you find that you overlooked something important.

Second, review your list of miscellaneous learning tasks and prioritize by assigning an A, a B, or a C to the left of each item. An A item is one that you must complete during the week, a B item is one that you want to accomplish during the week, and a C item is one that you know you will need to do eventually but is not necessary to finish that week. (You can change the time scale if you find that daily or biweekly or monthly lists work better for you, but it's best to start with making a weekly list and then modifying the time scale later, if necessary.)

Examine the list before you attempt to prioritize it. If you have all As, something is very wrong—you will be trying to put out fires all week long! Similarly, if you have all Cs, you may want to reexamine your priorities because not many students can let their studies slide for an entire week without getting something done. To do well with time management, you must learn to discriminate what needs to be done immediately from what can wait until later.

Third, try to apply your list for a week. Review the list each morning to see what you must do and what must be given priority. Each time you complete a task, check it off with a large, colored check mark (✓). You'll find that you enjoy checking off items. At the end of the week, you need to study what you've done. If you don't have all your A items checked off, you need to change the way that you schedule your study time; you must reserve time to do the As first. If you find that you have little or nothing checked off, you need to reconsider whether you are committed to meeting your goals as a student.

Sustained procrastination can be an indication that psychological problems are of more pressing concern than schoolwork. Procrastination is an almost irresistible subject for jokes. Perhaps you've heard the one about the Procrastinators Club meeting announcement: Come Whenever You Get Around to It. For some individuals, however, procrastination is no laughing matter. It is a serious problem that requires counseling.

For most students, overcoming procrastination will not require special help. With a little practice you will be able to use the Lakein ABC method to set up your learning jobs every week and adjust the time that you need to allocate for studying depending on the mix of As, Bs, and Cs that you have each week. You can modify the Lakein method by adding columns or pages for work activities as well as for home or recreational activities.

The reality is that anything you do not list as an A, a B, or a C activity automatically becomes a D activity—a default—something you consider so unimportant that it is not even listed among your priorities. Don't put off making your home or recreation list until you have finished all of your school and work activities. If you do, then home or play becomes a D activity. You could get straight As at school and flunk out at home.

Good Time Management Is Also Good Stress Management

You cannot be effective in juggling the tasks involved in the many roles that you have—student, worker, parent, housekeeper, citizen, spouse, and so forth— if you don't consciously make time for *everything* that is important in your life (see Chapter 5 for more help with balancing your multiple roles).

A basic difference between people who are happy and those who are not is the balance of positives to negatives that they have in their lives. Happier people have more positives and fewer negatives. Stress management depends on building up a robust ratio of positives to negatives so that when negatives inevitably enter your life there still is a buffer of positives to offset the negatives. This means that it is essential to include in your weekly listing of activities a number of guaranteed positives. In that way, you take control of your own happiness. It also is essential that when new negatives enter your life you add new positives. Don't just wait for the negatives to go away to return to "normal."

Stress management has shown that meaningfulness is one of the most powerful dimensions of personal life that can provide resistance to stress. People who feel that they contribute something meaningful to life more significant than their own egocentric needs are able to withstand extremely stressful negatives. In a small but important way, you can contribute to the meaningfulness of your life as a student by becoming a learner who seeks meanings from your studies beyond performing well on exams. Include enough time for activities that enlarge your role as a learner. Be sure to include tasks that take you beyond the assigned material into your own explorations as a learner.

THE STUDENT STRESSOR TEST

There is no doubt that being a student can be stressful, and adult reentry students can be exposed to considerable stress from many directions. It is healthy to pay attention to your stress level and to get help if you are experiencing excessive stress for a prolonged period of time. The Hart Student Stressor Test can be a useful self-screening device to detect if students are carrying undue amounts of stress as they try to perform in their courses.

Try taking it now and see how you score. Take the test again next term. If you score above the 90th percentile, and if your score stays there for several terms, you should definitely seek professional help.

Instructions: Rate the following items using a scale of 1 to 5, with 1 the anchor rating for "no stress" and 5 the anchor rating for an item that causes you "extreme stress." Be sure to rate every item.

_____   1. Personal appearance.
_____   2. Weight problems.
_____   3. Fear of war.
_____   4. Marital plans.
_____   5. Living arrangements.
_____   6. Problems with boyfriend/girlfriend/spouse.
_____   7. Personal problems with your immediate family.
_____   8. Drug/alcohol problems.
_____   9. Financial concerns (e.g., tuition, housing).

_____ 10. Lack of close friends.

_____ 11. Child-care concerns.

_____ 12. Pressures at work.

_____ 13. Lack of personal time for yourself.

_____ 14. Current job-searching plans.

_____ 15. Car/transportation problems.

_____ 16. Membership in campus organizations.

_____ 17. Speaking in public.

_____ 18. Test anxiety (exams and finals).

_____ 19. Difficulty in class scheduling when starting new terms.

_____ 20. Competition with other students and peer groups.

_____ 21. Grades.

_____ 22. Difficulties with an instructor.

_____ 23. Postgraduate plans.

_____ 24. My overall level of physical health now is 1, very good—no problems, to 5, very poor—many physical difficulties.

_____ 25. My overall stress level now is 1, very low, to 5, very high.

Scoring: Add your ratings for items #1 through #23. A score of 48 is average, placing you at the 50th percentile for students in the normative group. A score of 40 is at the 25th percentile. 56 is at the 75th percentile. 66 is at the 90th percentile and may indicate serious stress problems if it persists. Also, pay attention to your scores on items #24 and #25. If either one is rated at the 5 level, you may still be at risk even if your overall score on the Student Stressor Test is not high.

READING GUIDES

Mortimer Adler, philosopher and Great Books Program founder, distinguished between reading for information and reading for understanding. He identified four levels of reading: _elementary reading, inspectional reading, analytical reading,_ and _syntopical reading. Elementary reading_ is simply trying to comprehend the words in a book, _inspectional reading_ is skimming or scanning, _analytical reading_ is the reading that most students are attempting most of the time with textbooks, and _syntopical reading_ is an advanced form of reading that must be done when critiquing a book or developing a thesis or paper that draws from several books.

Adler identified what he called *the essence of active reading* in four basic questions that a reader asks and tries to answer for expository or nonfiction works:

1. What is the book about as a whole? (Identify the leading theme of the book and the essential subordinate themes or topics.)
2. What is being said in detail and how? (Discover the author's main ideas, assertions, and arguments.)
3. Is the book true in whole or part? (Make some effort to evaluate whether the author's views are true.)
4. What of it? (What difference does the information or understanding that you obtain from the book make to you, and why does the author believe it is important?)

Adler believes these four questions "summarize the whole obligation of the reader. They apply to anything worth reading—a book or an article or even an advertisement."*

Adler's questions may seem rather lofty and removed from the kind of reading tasks that most students undertake when they attempt to study a textbook. Most students never ask the third and fourth questions. They certainly are beyond what is ordinarily applied in the SQ4R study method presented earlier. However, reading that gets you through lower-division, introductory courses is not the kind of reading that will be necessary in advanced courses that require you to perform your own research and synthesize information and ideas from several sources. All too often, students restrict their reading to textbook reading and do not know how to read in a wider, deeper way. It is very important to learn to read at many levels and to recognize that there is a more advanced level of reading than what is required to simply read well enough from texts to pass exams.

Real education will continue for a lifetime, and you will read more than textbooks after you leave college. Students need to understand that textbooks are compilations of information and ideas from primary sources. Primary sources are articles, chapters, monographs, and books that are not organized in the way that textbooks are usually organized. Students are advised to consult at least one additional textbook (and preferably several) beyond the text that is assigned for the course. Students are often astounded to learn that what one textbook author pre-

---

*Adler, M. and Van Doren, M. *How to Read a Book*. New York: Simon and Schuster, 1972.

TIP	Use Shorthand

Reading and questioning will become second nature if you make up your own shorthand set of symbols to write in the margins of your books or on stick-on notes for library books. Such symbols are especially helpful if you need to do book reviews because they can be assembled into a rough draft.

sents as the core of a subject is not even mentioned by a different author. Both authors are supposedly presenting the "same subject."

WRITING PAPERS

All good writing is usually rewriting! Students sometimes believe that they should write perfect and complete papers on their first drafts, but that is not realistic. Unfortunately, this approach to writing is perpetuated because students are exposed in high school mostly to timed, short essay exams for which they need to write a good draft on their one and only attempt. But even in exam situations, you should leave a little time before you start writing to map out what you will write and in what order. Leave a little time at the end to proofread what you've written for spelling, grammar, and meaningfulness.

The blank page often intimidates poor writers, just as empty pots and pans and a refrigerator full of groceries would intimidate inexperienced cooks. But writing is easier than cooking. You can fill a page with doodles to get started, expand the doodles into a concept map, expand that into an outline, and then do a first draft that can be revised repeatedly. It is very difficult to make a poorly cooked omelet better, but you can convert poor writing into good writing with enough revisions. Some people view writing a book as an impossible task, an act of genius. They see a 300-page book as 300 blank pages that had to be filled in word by word, line by line without stopping from beginning to end. Of course, 300-page books are written just like 300-mile journeys are walked—step by step, with a mental map of what it takes to get from one place to another. The same people who are overwhelmed and intimidated by blank pages may be able to take an auto engine apart and reassemble it, or navigate a boat trip, or cook a five-course meal for a banquet without hesitation.

Tɪᴘ	Use Models

A recommendation for aspiring writers is to keep a folder of excerpts from writers whom you admire. Make it an eclectic collection, including everything from newspaper articles to comic book dialogues to screenplays to textbook samples. Once you have a few models, you can choose one that comes closest to the writing task that you need to accomplish and then measure whatever you write against that model. You gradually will internalize the model, and you'll no longer need to have it at hand when you write.

The same skills that are involved in effective reading are useful for effective writing. Indeed, it is impossible to be a fine writer without being an accomplished reader. That's because you must learn to appreciate good writing as a reader before you can effectively criticize your own writing and guide your rewrites. One reason few students begin college as effective writers is that they are not effective readers at the syntopical level.

Let's consider the practical steps that are involved when you are fulfilling a typical writing assignment. Imagine that you need to write a 10- to 15-page midterm exam for an upper-division course. What do you need to do? Here are some suggestions:

1. Carefully study the way the instructor has described the assignment. Don't write a paper that doesn't cover what the instructor asked for. For example: An instruction to "summarize and compare the theories of learning that are covered in your textbook" is quite different from an instruction to "summarize and compare the theories of learning that were extant in the 1940s in the field of psychology." You will need to go to the library and collect some resources about psychology in the 1940s to fulfill the second assignment; doing the first assignment simply involves careful analytical reading of your textbook. Similarly, an instruction to "summarize and compare" is quite different from an instruction to "compare and speculate about the importance of" different theories of learning. Your instructor may also give you specific guidelines about the format you should use for references, footnotes, and citations. If not, be sure to pick your own style guide and stay with it—don't skip from one format to another.

2. Apply the skill you now know from studying and reading— doodling. You will write better if you start putting things on paper, and your first jottings do not need to be complete sentences in complete paragraphs.

3. Compile the resources that you will draw on in your writing. These may include lecture notes, reading notes, articles, chapters, books—anything that you can use to think about the subject or that will provide facts and quotes.

4. Begin to sketch an outline. Your outline just puts into words your doodle map. Don't worry if the outline is very sketchy at first. It has to be. Those elaborate outlines that you sometimes see in textbooks were written *after* the book was drafted, not *before*.

5. Begin to write the rough draft of the paper, and try to find a voice that works to convey your thoughts and meet the instructions of the assignment. Finding the voice is as important as finding the main points that you will express. For example, an informal, first-person voice may not work at all for some assignments ("I think Newton's first law is cool.") but will fit very well for other assignments (e.g., the classic high school English assignment "tell about your summer vacation").

6. Push the rough draft to completion. At this stage, you are trying to get from the beginning through the middle and to the end of the paper. Don't worry now about logic, grammar, spelling, and punctuation. You are concerned with bulk production. Your goal now is to get a first product that can then be revised and revised again.

7. Put your rough draft aside for at least several hours before attempting a revision. You want to return to the draft with fresh eyes and fresh ideas.

8. Go through the rough draft and begin to correct it for spelling, punctuation, and grammar. Feel free to move sections and make notes where you need to add new sections. Be bold and delete what doesn't seem to fit or make sense. (There's an old saying that a writer's best friend is a large wastebasket.) However, do keep copies of your original versions so that you can go back and retrieve something that you deleted should you decide later that it can be used.

TIP	First Drafts

Some writers do very long first drafts and then shorten; others do very brief first drafts and then expand. If your first draft for a 15-page paper turns out to be 30 pages, that's fine; if it's 3 pages, that's fine too. Do whatever works for you!

TIP	Keep the Reader in Mind

Before you do the writing of the final draft, apply the SQ4R and I CARE methods to your own writing. Does it make sense? Would someone who reads what you've written learn something? Have you organized what you want to convey into sections that make it easy for the reader? Have you been an effective teacher for the reader? As you rewrite for the final draft, keep the reader in mind. You are not writing just for yourself; your instructor will be reading your paper and perhaps other students as well.

9. Prepare the second draft, again pushing through to completion. If you get stuck revising a certain section, make a note in the margin to return to it later; don't get stalled.

10. Again put the draft aside and return to it later before you attempt to rewrite.

11. Complete the final draft. You must finish everything, even difficult sections that were left incomplete in the second draft. For most school papers, three drafts will be sufficient; for special papers such as senior capstones or theses, you may need to do more than three.

12. Proofread what you consider your final draft. Be sure to use all the tools that may be built into your word processor.

13. After all this work, be sure to print a copy of your paper with adequate margins and clear, clean printing. Always keep a copy for yourself; originals do get lost, so you need both an electronic and a print backup.

These 13 steps to good writing will not make you a Hemingway or a Shakespeare, but they will give you a basis for writing that can be used again and again in your course work and later in your career. Be sure to continue your explorations of writing by consulting the online resources that are available at the Guide's website. The Web links contain everything from style guides to grammar checkers to more how-to-write guidelines.

Avoiding Plagiarism

A simple rule to keep in mind is that anything you copy from elsewhere should be quoted and cited, and that anything you paraphrase from someone else should be identified as coming from another

> ### TIP | Check Spelling and Grammar
>
> If your word processor has a spell checker, be sure to use it. Also use a dictionary when you are not sure if a word should be changed. Your word processor may also include an outliner, which will let you see what your chapter looks like in full sentence outline form; that's a good tool to use to examine the logical structure of your paper. Some word processors include a thesaurus function, so you can look for alternate words if you notice that you are repeating the same word too frequently. Many word processors also have a grammar checker; use that too, but use it cautiously because grammar checkers are not as accurate as spell checkers and you need to know a good deal about grammar to decide whether a recommended change is appropriate. Never make a change just because the grammar checker suggests it; understand what is being suggested.

source. Instructors don't want you to avoid citing, quoting, and paraphrasing. They do want you to be explicit about what is yours and what is drawn from someone else.

A very effective psychological test is used to detect plagiarism at a number of major universities, including the Armed Services Academies. The test is based on the psychological finding that a writer can easily reproduce his own writing but will have great difficulty reproducing someone else's writing. Students who are accused of plagiarism are asked to reproduce a section of the paper that they submitted as their own. If the student can closely reproduce the section, then the odds are extremely high that the student did indeed write the original paper. If the student cannot reproduce the original, the odds are equally high that the section was plagiarized.

TESTS AND OTHER ANXIETIES

Everyone who's ever taken an important test knows what it's like to feel "test anxiety," but some students find tests more intimidating than others do. In general, the best ways to cope with test anxiety are to (1) acquire effective study skills, (2) practice effective time management so that you are prepared for each test, and (3) know yourself as a learner and test taker so that you understand what helps and what hinders your performance in a testing situation.

Test preparation will vary depending on the kind of test that you will be taking, but everything you apply from your knowledge of study skills will contribute to your overall test preparation.

Test-Taking Skills for the Off-Campus Student

Here are some specific test-preparation tips adapted from study skills handouts used with adult students:

- Find out from the beginning of the course how much material each test will cover—a chapter at a time, accumulative as you go along? Will the final test be comprehensive (over the entire book), everything covered in the book after a certain point, everything covered in the course (including lectures), or restricted to a certain topic?

- Find out what percentage of your total course grade the test will contribute. You need to weight your study time accordingly.

- Try to find out what type of test will be given; your instructor may not specify the format. Some tests include a variety of types of questions (short answer, short essay, multiple choice, fill in the blank, true/false).

- Start the test by reading the instructions carefully; do not jump into answering questions as fast as you can.

- Don't rush through the test; pace yourself so you don't run out of time, but use all the allotted time that you need. Check over your test carefully after finishing.

- In essay exams, read all the questions before answering any. Then do some brief outline planning before answering. Write legibly so your instructor will not have to struggle to discern your words; forcing the instructor to decipher words will distract from your meanings. Try to avoid any spelling or grammatical errors, and be sure to leave time for proofreading your answers before turning in the exam. Always be sure when you reread your answers that you answered all of the questions asked.

- In multiple choice questions, read all the choices before answering. As in true/false questions, be very cautious on all questions that use inclusive/exclusive words such as *always* or *never*.

Specific techniques can help you avoid test anxiety or cope with it when it happens. The old familiar advice "count to 100," or "take deep breaths," or "think of a beautiful scene that you like" is not bad advice to apply when you feel the jitters approaching. However, it is much more effective to actually practice a relaxation or meditation technique so that you will know how it works and can apply it before you get into a test-taking situation. One such technique is "mantra meditation," described in the accompanying box.

Mantra Meditation

Cardiologist Herbert Benson has done a series of research studies showing that the centuries-old practice of mantra meditation can be learned and applied effectively to lower tension, pulse rate, and blood pressure. Here's how to do mantra meditation. Start by picking a word or sound that you like, something that's easy to pronounce like "aahh," "ing," "oooh," or "ohm"—the meaning of the word is not important because all you want is a word or sound that you can easily repeat. Then set aside 10 minutes or so every day so you can sit quietly with your eyes closed and repeat the word over and over to yourself. Hear the word repeating inside your head. Of course, you will find that all sorts of thoughts and images intrude on your effort to do nothing except repeat your mantra. That's okay—simply start repeating the word or sound again as soon as you notice that you've been

distracted. After practicing this meditation technique for a week, you should notice a definite quieting of your body and thoughts when you apply your mantra.

The way to use this technique in a test situation is to spend 5 or 10 minutes before you go into the testing room applying your mantra meditation. You should find that you are much less likely to get "speedy" and panicked during the test if you settle yourself down before the test begins.

Math Anxiety

A special form of anxiety that afflicts many students is math anxiety. For many students, difficulty with mathematical word problems stem from poor reading rather than poor skills in manipulating symbols. The Learning Services Centre at Cambrian College employs six steps to help students solve problems. Having the steps as a reference will help you develop good habits and keep you from freezing up in exams.

SIX STEPS IN SOLVING A PROBLEM

1. **Read the problem carefully.** Pay careful attention to wording. Underline key words and phrases. Don't mistake words that look similar but are not.
2. **Read the problem again.** See exactly what is given; see what values or numbers are provided.
3. **See what principles apply.** Every problem involves the application of certain principles or formulas, sometimes only one very simple one, maybe several. It is particularly important when studying courses that employ formulas, laws, rules, and so forth not only to memorize them in their symbolic form, but to understand the principles underlying their use and to be able to formulate them in your own words whenever possible.
4. **See how to apply the formula or principle.** If the problem is fairly obvious, note what must be done first, then second, and so on. Occasionally, when there is a choice of procedures, use the one that appears simplest and most direct.
5. **Carefully apply the principles and reach the solution.** The word *carefully* is of maximum importance here. A large percentage of errors and lost marks are the result of carelessness.
6. **Check your work.** See whether the answer seems sensible, and check each computation.

Pay careful attention to the sixth step. A characteristic of "innumeracy" is that some people do not apply good sense to numbers and math problems in the way that they certainly would to other problems of everyday life. Instead, they simply follow formulas without really thinking about what they mean or what would be a sensible range for an answer and what would be outside a sensible range.

There are a number of excellent books available to help students overcome math anxiety and achieve numeracy. If you are taking math or math-dependent courses and are worried about your ability to do well, consult one or more of these books and try to arrange to work with a math tutor. Tutoring in math and the sciences is a well-accepted practice, but students at a distance from a campus often are deprived of the benefits of tutoring. If possible, try to arrange for long-distance tutoring, which will show immediate and long-term benefits.

COMPUTER AND INTERNET LITERACY

Contemporary college students need to do more than use a pencil or pen; they must also be effective computer users and skilled Internet searchers. Detailed guidance in these areas was provided in Chapters 3 and 4. You should also check the library services, computer services, and learning center services of your institution for more guidance about how to use computers and utilize Web resources (visit in person if the institution is accessible to you, but also look up the websites for these offices). The website for this Guide lists a plenitude of resources from libraries, computer centers, and learning centers collected from many fine colleges and universities.

The most important single fact for a student to realize about the Web is that it provides the biggest university and the biggest library in the world. When you take a course—any course—you can go to the Web and find out how that course is being taught at other colleges and universities. You can find lecture notes, lab exercises, audio lectures, exams, simulations, multimedia displays, interactive learning exercises, and all the other tools for learning. No modern student should ever take a course from a single teacher when it is possible to go to websites and find the instructional resources from many teachers for the same course. Make it a habit when you orient yourself to a new course to visit the Web and find at least one or two examples of how that course is being taught elsewhere.

We've all experienced listening to one person explain an idea only to "not get it" and then listening to another person explain the same idea and have everything become clear. The passage from not getting it to getting it, from not knowing to knowing, from ignorance to understanding is available to every student, or should be. No student should be dependent on one teacher and, with the growth of online instructional repositories, no student needs to be narrowly restricted to one presentation of a subject. A student at Anywhere College can see how calculus is taught at Everywhere University. A student at Anywhere College can examine the syllabi, quizzes, lecture notes, exams, learning objects, and teaching tools from courses around the world. The EduResources Portal (see DLGUIDE website) lists collections of instructional resources (including complete courses) from colleges, universities, and organizations worldwide. Check the DLGUIDE website for access to repository collections of instructional resources. Here are just two examples: the MIT OpenCourseWare Project is designed to provide complete course materials for *all* the MIT courses; the MERLOT project includes a huge collection of instructional resources (organized by subject area) from a multitude of institutions. Access to these online instructional resources will be important to you as an enrolled student at your institution and will become even more important to you when you graduate and wish to continue your education as a lifelong learner.

SOME FINAL TIPS FOR BECOMING A BETTER STUDENT

Here are several tips that will help you become a more effective learner—not just in distance learning classes but in any classroom or out-of-class learning project that you wish to undertake:

- Take the time to read some how-to-study books available in libraries and bookstores and online. Check our website for some references. As with everything else, you need to select the techniques and ideas that work for you.

- Make a one-, two-, and three-year learning plan that lists, term by term, what you intend to study and how each course or project will contribute to your overall learning goals. Having a long-range plan will help you persist in those courses and assignments that are not inherently interesting but do relate to your goals. You may need to consult with your advisor to assemble the full plan, but sketch it out right away so that you have at least a general picture of when you will take which course and understand why each course is a part of your program.

- Use the ABC time management method at least one full term for your work, personal, and study life. Once you have used this method for a term, you're likely to continue to use it, at least whenever you are working under time pressures.

- Keep a study diary for a week. Recording how you feel when doing assignments, reading textbooks, writing papers, solving problems, and taking tests will tell you a lot about how you approach a learning task and function as a learner.

- Find a study buddy. Research has demonstrated that it helps to study with someone else, especially in those courses that require extensive problem solving, such as mathematics, statistics, accounting, and science. If you are not meeting other students directly in class, arrange to communicate with your study partner via the telephone or email.

- Make an effort to meet with your instructors right away. You don't have to say anything profound or ask a difficult question—just begin to communicate. Once you start, it will be easier to ask for help when you really need it.

- Find something in the news that relates to what you are studying in each of your courses. It is important to take what you learn outside the textbooks and make connections to everyday life. Try talking with a friend or relative about what you are learning and explain how it connects to events in the news.

- Pretend that you are the instructor for the next chapter that you read. The most effective way to learn something is to "teach" it. Once you have prepared a short lecture and a short quiz that covers the chapter, you'll be approaching the subject from the active mind of an instructor, as a communicator and an organizer, rather than from the passive mind of a passive student.

- Apply one of the learning theories that have been mentioned in this chapter to your own efforts as a learner. Check the associated website for more information.

- Browse through the instructional resources available at some of the major instructional repositories such as MIT's OpenCourseWare or MERLOT or at referatories such as the EduResources Portal. By getting familiar with these resources in advance you'll be equipped to supplement the materials that are assigned for your courses with additional resources that will help you to learn better and learn more in any course that you take.

- Reward yourself! Studying shouldn't be a dreaded grind. By treating yourself well as a student, you become a better student. By rewarding yourself with music, food, play, art, or whatever you choose, you can look forward to learning rather than dreading the time that you spend studying. Eventually, learning will become rewarding, and you will have changed your role or image as a student. In one view, this entire chapter has been about helping you make this shift. Learn for yourself, for pleasure, and to gain understanding versus learning for others, from fear, by trying to memorize.

Questions to Ask Distance Education Providers

Here are some straightforward questions to ask the institutional representatives where you are planning to take courses or pursue a degree (see Chapter 2 for additional and related questions).

1 *What tutoring services are available for distance learning students in the specific course that I'm planning to take? How do the tutoring services that are available for distance learning students compare with those for on-campus students?*

2 *Are instructors available by phone and/or email to answer questions that emerge from the lectures or the readings?*

3 *What is the student–teacher ratio for this course?*

4 *Is the instructor for this course a regular faculty member or a student assistant? Has the instructor taught the course before? Does the instructor teach the course on campus as well as off campus?*

5 *Can I view the syllabus for the course so that I will know about the requirements and grading before I take the course?*

6 *Is there information available about how students who have taken this course have evaluated the course and the instructor?*

7 *Will I have a single faculty advisor who will help me plan my degree program of courses and help me progress through the program?*

Not every distance learning institution will have a complete answer for every one of these questions, but the better ones will have satisfactory answers for at least some of the questions and will always be concerned about helping students do as well as they can in their courses.

SUMMARY: JUST A BEGINNING!

There is no conclusion to learning or to learning about learning. What you've acquired in this chapter is just a beginning that can be applied and extended as you use these study ideas and methods in different courses. You should try other approaches, devise your own, and reflect on your own growth as a learner. The person who has become a self-guided learner is capable of changing mere information into meaningful and useful ideas.

As educator Carl Rogers stated, in quoting one of his own teachers, "Don't be a damn ammunition wagon, be a rifle." One of the greatest needs in our information age is for learners who can emerge from being information consumers to information evaluators and informed knowledge creators. At this level, learning becomes an art. Welcome to the never-ending art of learning!

www.DLGuide.info

Visit this website for additional information and activities.

Final Word

When we hear the term *pioneer*, we may think of the great events of history, such as Columbus's voyages to the New World or the first space flight to the moon. On a smaller scale, though, you are among those pioneers. You have entered the brave new world of "virtual higher education."

This book has been your guide on this new journey. Rather than having a human navigator to help you avoid the rocks and shoals of the trip, you have had a "virtual team" of guides who have given you a dynamic map of this new educational world.

Because distance learning is new and dynamic, it is also very exciting. Where our traditional campus and classroom structures have been in place for hundreds of years, distance learning is emerging rapidly as a new educational culture. This culture departs dramatically from the classroom-based educational structure that we have all experienced. And, of greatest importance, rather than the professor being at the center of this new instructional process, you, the learner, are now at the center.

All of this discussion about distance learning and the ways in which it is different from traditional learning should not lead you to conclude that classrooms and professors are being replaced. Quite the opposite is true. Distance learning is changing the scope and scale of education. By using electronic technologies, it is expanding the size of the classroom (by sending education beyond the classroom walls), and it is extending the reach of professors to learners (wherever they are located) by providing a variety of distance learning options.

This Guide has provided you with a detailed introduction to this new world of distance learning and a variety of navigational tools to help you on your educational journey. Chapter 1 introduced you to distance learning and Chapter 2 told you who provides it. Chapters 3 and 4 provided detailed information about the two tools most critical to your success—the computer and the virtual library. Chapters 5 and 6 provided information and advice about how to be a successful student and how to maintain balance in your life as you are learning.

Of most importance, the Guide has emphasized that your educational journey never ends. Your new skills for learning in an electronic and virtual world will be used repeatedly as you return to education—to expand your horizons, to remain current in your career, or as you develop new skills to help you change jobs or careers a number of times in your working life. As you access learning in future years, return and visit us. You may have missed some things of interest on your first trip. We look forward to being your navigator in the future in the ever-changing world of distance learning!

Index